A-Z EXE...

C000198135

CONTENTS

REFERENCE

Motorway	M5	Car Park (Selected)	P
A Road	A30	Park & Ride	Sowton P+🚌
B Road	B3212	Church or Chapel	†
Dual Carriageway		Cycleway	🚲
One-way Street		Fire Station	■
Traffic flow on A Roads is also indicated by a heavy line on the driver's left.	→	Hospital	H
Restricted Access		House Numbers Selected roads	13 8 3
Pedestrianized Road		Information Centre	i
Track & Footpath		National Grid Reference	^{3}75
Residential Walkway		Police Station	▲
Railway	Station Tunnel Level Crossing	Post Office	★
		Toilet	▽
		with facilities for the Disabled	▽
Built-up Area	WEST ST.	Educational Establishment	▢
Local Authority Boundary	— · — · —	Hospital or Hospice	▢
Posttown Boundary	— — —	Industrial Building	▢
Postcode Boundary within Posttown	— — —	Leisure or Recreational Facility	▢
Map Continuation	16	Place of Interest	▢
	Large Scale City Centre 4	Public Building	▢
		Shopping Centre or Market	▢
		Other Selected Buildings	▢

SCALE

Map Pages 6-45   1:15840   Map Pages 4-5   1:7920

0   ¼   ½ Mile   0   ⅛   ¼ Mile

0   250   500   750 Metres   0   100   200   300   400 Metres

4 inches (10.16 cm) to 1 mile   6.31 cm to 1 km   8 inches (20.32cm) to 1 mile   12.63 cm to 1 km

Copyright of Geographers' A-Z Map Company Limited

Head Office :
Fairfield Road, Borough Green, Sevenoaks, Kent TN15 8PP
Telephone: 01732 781000 (Enquiries & Trade Sales)
              01732 783422 (Retail Sales)
www.a-zmaps.co.uk
Copyright © Geographers' A-Z Map Co. Ltd.

OS Ordnance Survey® This product includes mapping data licensed from Ordnance Survey® with the permission of the Controller of Her Majesty's Stationery Office.

© Crown Copyright 2003. All rights reserved. Licence number 100017302

Edition 3 2004,   Edition 3A 2005 (Part Revision)

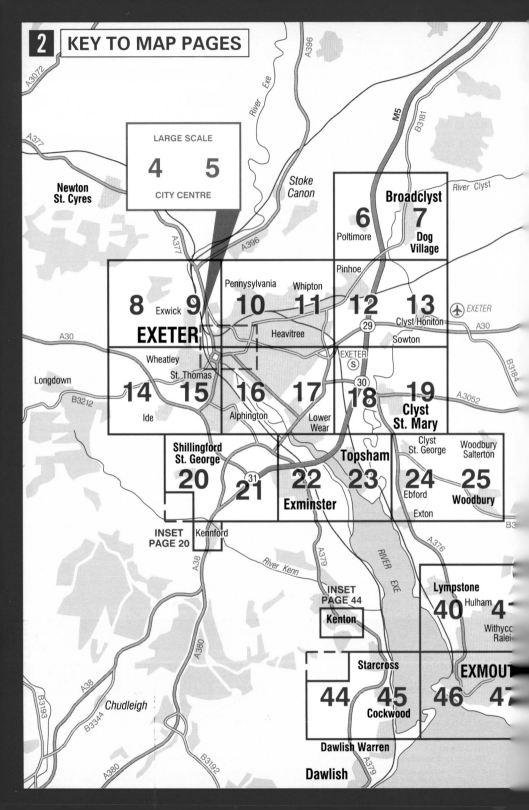

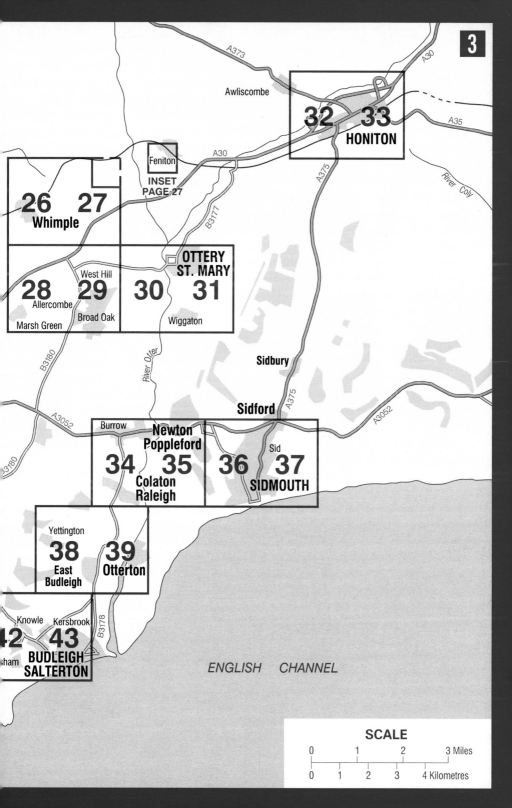

3

Awliscombe

A373

A30

A35

River Coly

32 **33**
HONITON

A375

Feniton

INSET PAGE 27

26 **27**
Whimple

B3177

OTTERY ST. MARY

West Hill

28 **29** **30** **31**

Allercombe

Broad Oak

Wiggaton

Marsh Green

B3180

River Otter

Sidbury

Sidford

A375

A3052

A3052

B3180

Burrow

Newton Poppleford

Sid

34 **35** **36** **37**

Colaton Raleigh **SIDMOUTH**

Yettington

38 **39**

East Budleigh **Otterton**

Knowle   Kersbrook

B3178

2 **43**

ham

BUDLEIGH SALTERTON

ENGLISH   CHANNEL

SCALE

| 0 | 1 | 2 | 3 Miles |

| 0 | 1 | 2 | 3 | 4 Kilometres |

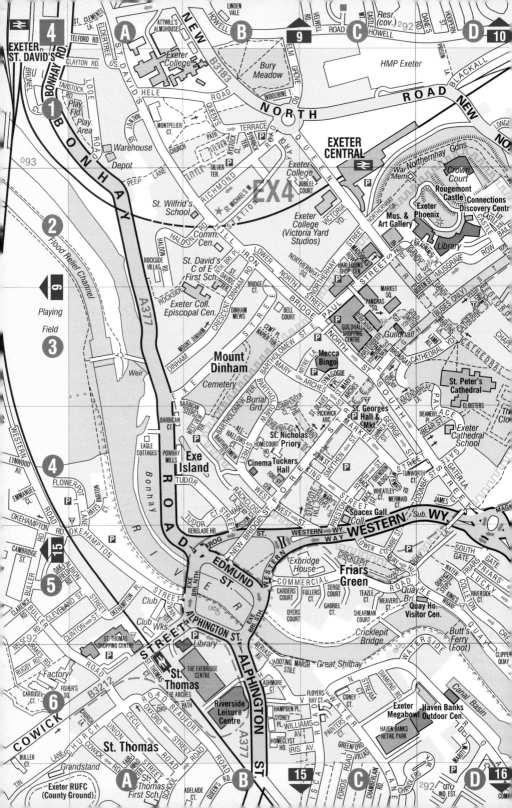

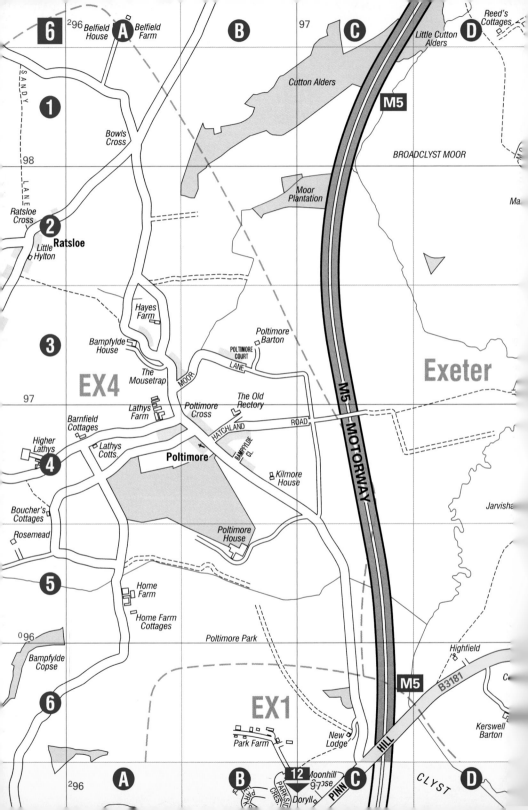

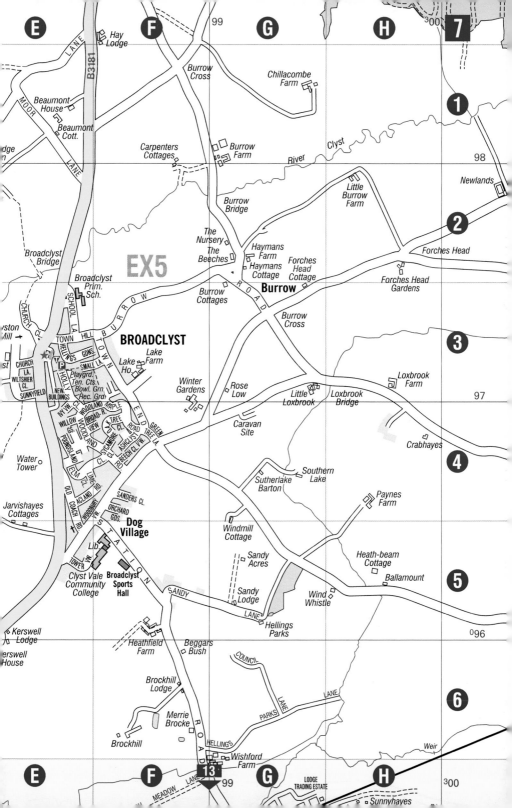

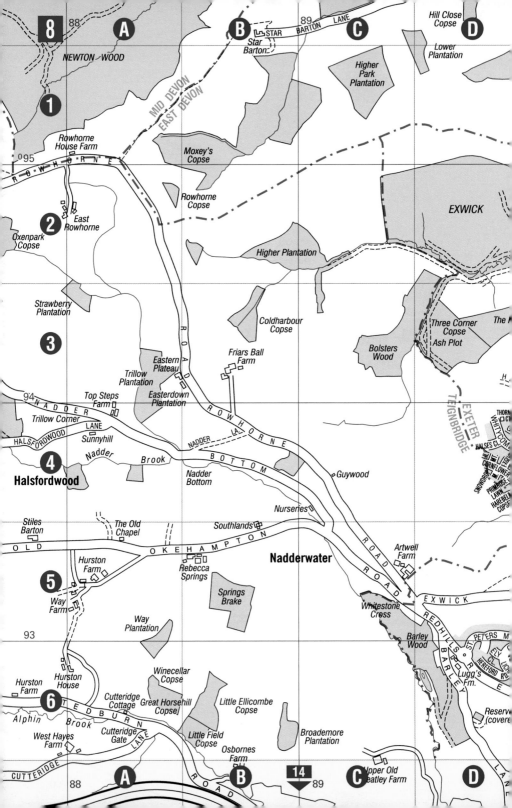

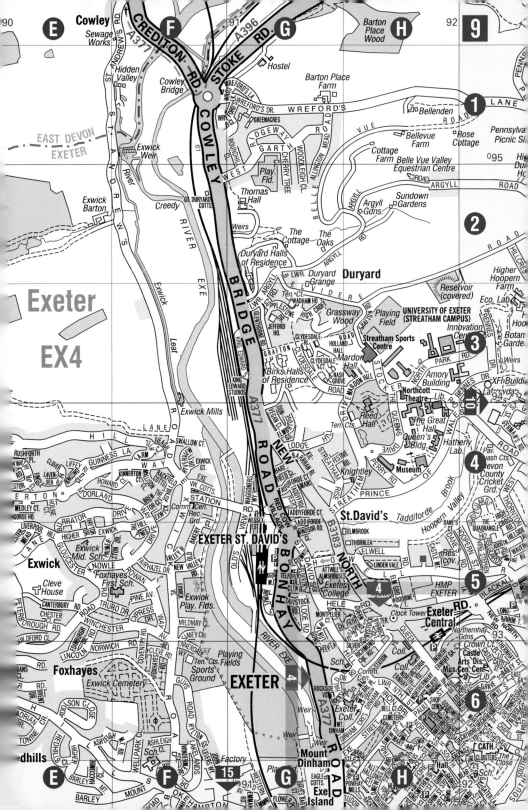

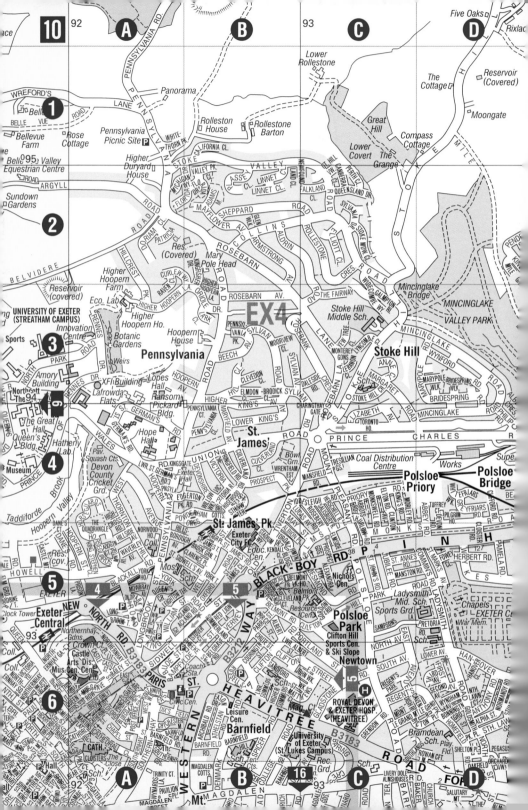

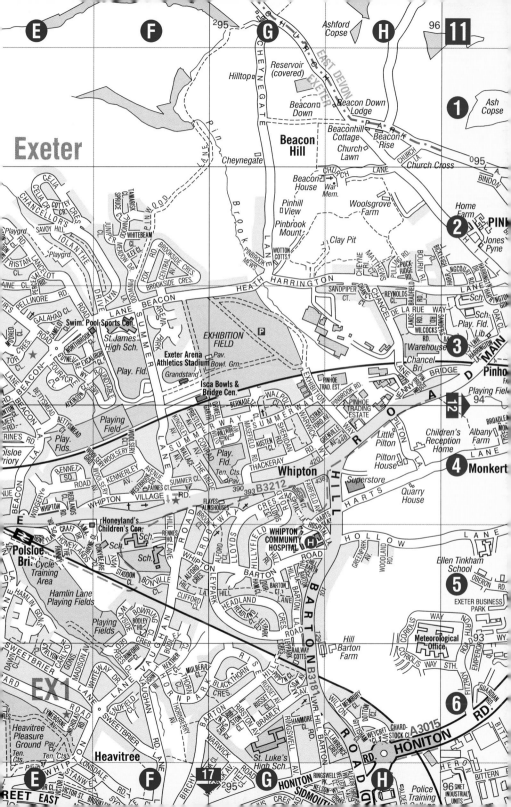

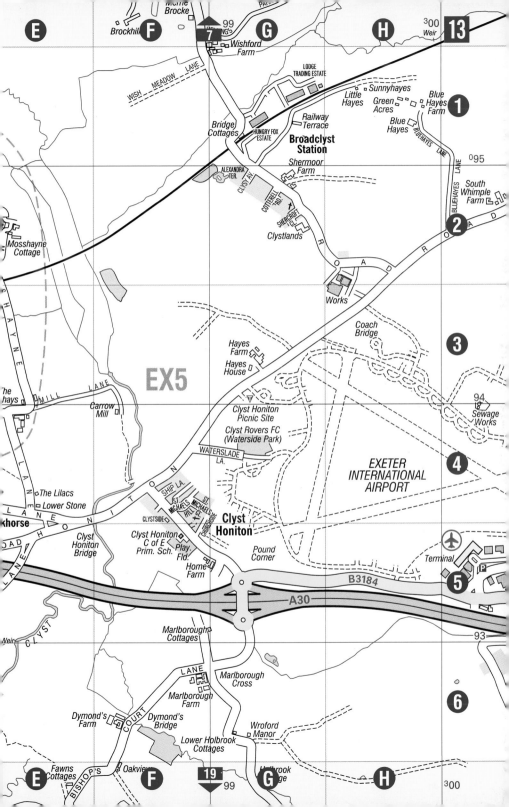

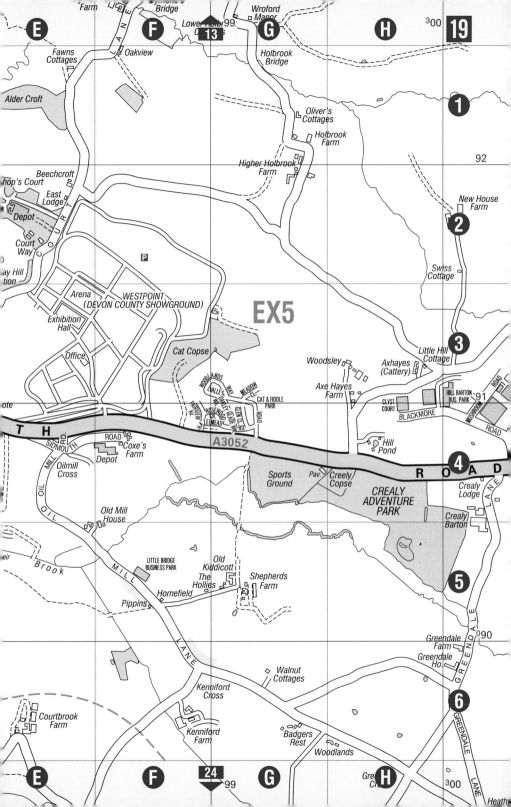

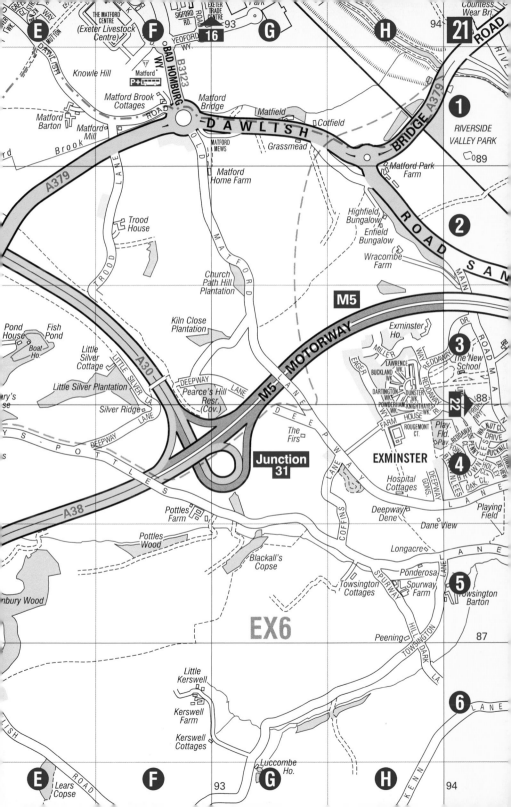

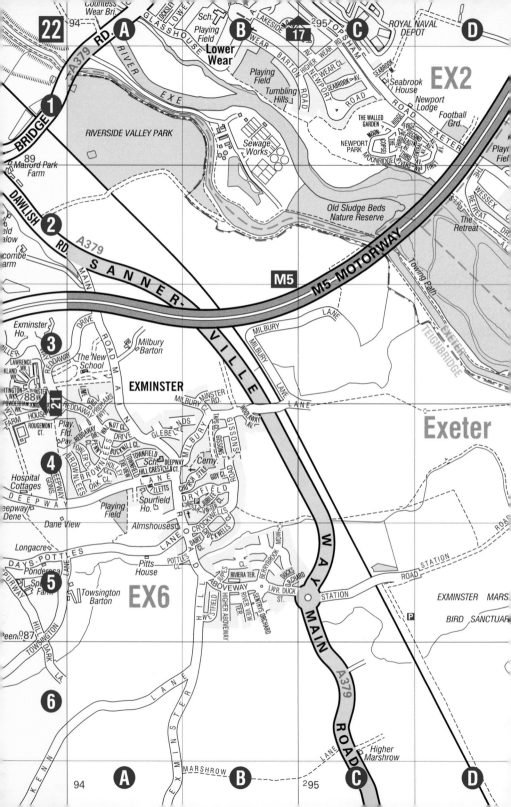

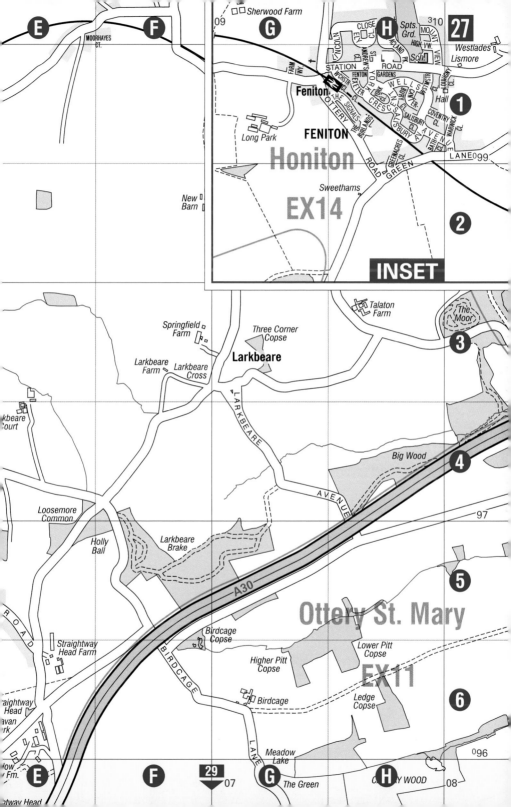

E F G H

Sherwood Farm

Spts. Grd.

310

CLOSE

MOUNT

ST. ANDREW'S CL.

ACLAND PK.

HIGH VW.

Westlades

Lismore

FARM WY.

WORSTER RD.

STATION

FENTON CT.

EXETER CL.

YORK GARDENS

ROAD

WELLS

Sch.

COVENTRY CL.

Hall

Feniton

THE SIGNALS RD.

SALISBURY

SALISBURY AV.

WARWICK CL.

FENITON

OTTERY

BATH CL.

1

Long Park

GREENACRES CL.

LANE 099

New Barn

FENITON

GREEN

Honiton

Sweethams

EX14

2

INSET

MOORHAYES CT.

09

Talaton Farm

The Moor

Springfield Farm

Three Corner Copse

3

Larkbeare Farm

Larkbeare

Larkbeare Cross

L A R K B E A R E

kbeare Court

Big Wood

4

A V E N U E

Loosemore Common

97

Holly Ball

Larkbeare Brake

A30

5

Ottery St. Mary

R O A D

Birdcage Copse

Lower Pitt Copse

Straightway Head Farm

Higher Pitt Copse

EX11

B I R D C A G E

Birdcage

Ledge Copse

6

aightway Head

avan rk

L A N E

Meadow Lake

096

ow Fm.

E F G H

htway Head

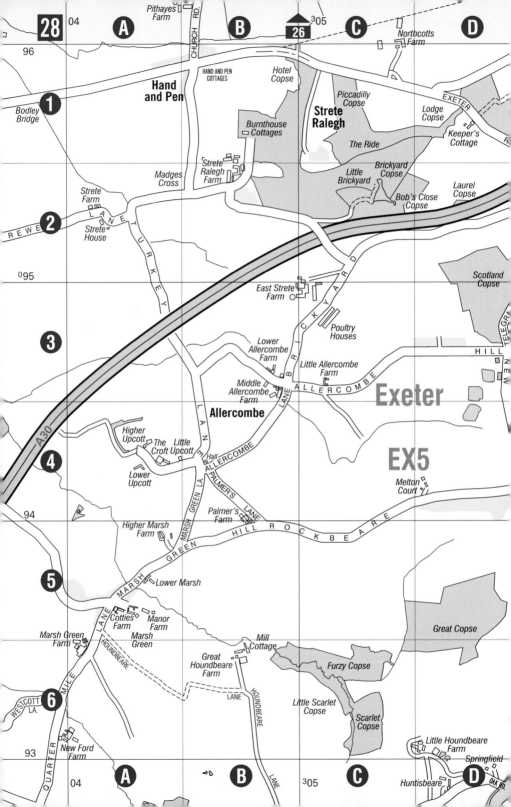

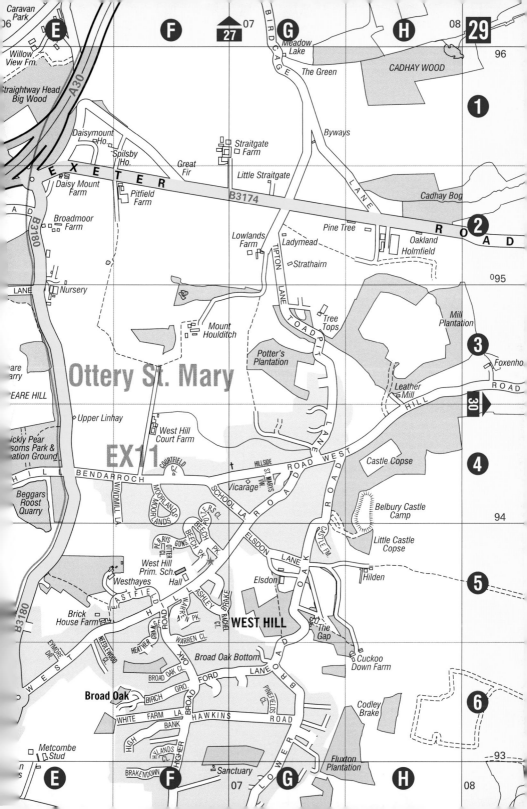

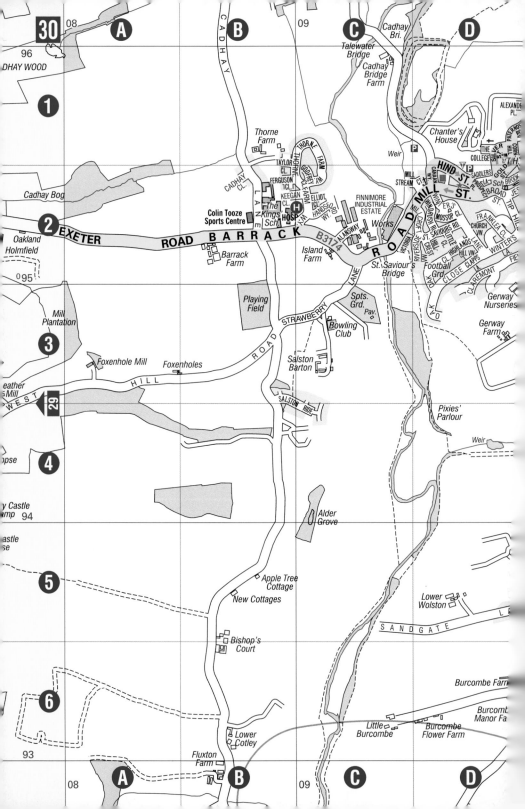

08
96

A   **B**   CADHAY   09   **C**   Cadhay Bri.   **D**

DHAY WOOD

Talewater Bridge

Cadhay Bridge Farm

1

Chanter's House

ALEXANDER PL.

THE COLLEGE

Cadhay Bog

Thorne Farm

Weir

P

SILVER HILL

PATERSON'S

SADDLERS

HIND ST.

MILL STREAM

ST.

BROAD ST.

TIP

TAYLOR CL.

THORNE FARM LANE

GODREY CL. FARM

FERGUSON CL.

CADHAY CL.

KEEGAN CL.

The Kings Sch.

H HOSP.

ELLIOT CL.

HANDSEL WY.

FINNIMORE INDUSTRIAL ESTATE

ROAD

MILL

WINDPOST WY.

MOSSOP CL.

ST. SAVIOURS RD.

FRANKLEA CL.

CHURCH VW.

WINTER'S

2 EXETER ROAD BARRACK

Oakland Holmfield

Barrack Farm

Island Farm

B3174

ALANSWAY

Works

St. Saviour's Bridge

VICTORIA RD.

RIVERSIDE WY.

CL. CREST

CL. HIGHLANDS

MILL VW.

CLOSE CLAPPS

Football Grd.

OAK

CLAREMONT LA. FIE

95

Mill Plantation

Playing Field

ROAD

STRAWBERRY

Spts. Grd. Pav.

Gerway Nurseries

Gerway Farm

3

eather s Mill

Foxenhole Mill

Foxenholes

HILL

Bowling Club

Salston Barton

OAK

WEST **29**

SALSTON RIDE

Pixies' Parlour

Weir

4

y Castle amp 94

astle se

Alder Grove

5

Apple Tree Cottage

New Cottages

Lower Wolston

SANDGATE

LA

pse

6

Bishop's Court

Lower Cotley

Fluxton Farm

Little Burcombe

Burcombe Flower Farm

Burcombe Farm

Burcomb Manor Fa

93
08

A   **B**   09   **C**   **D**

Colin Tooze Sports Centre

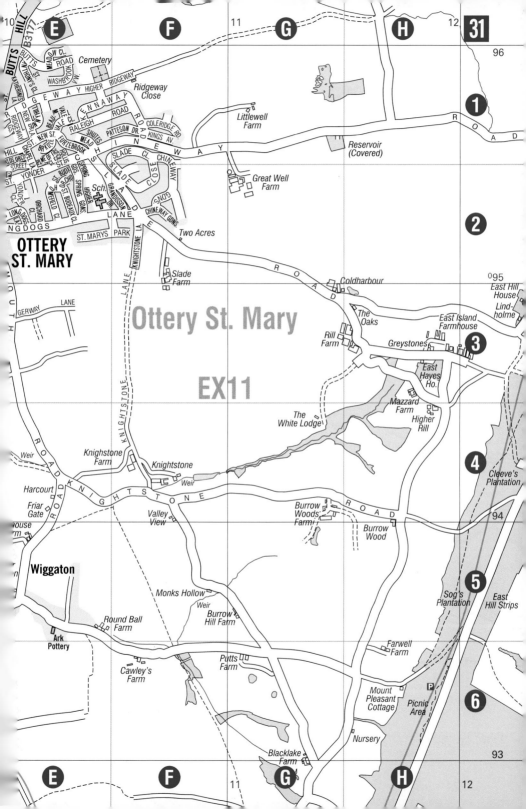

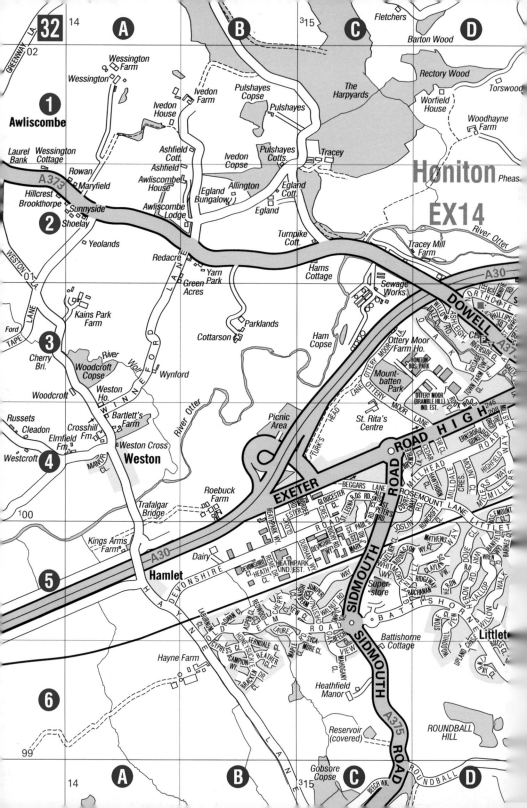

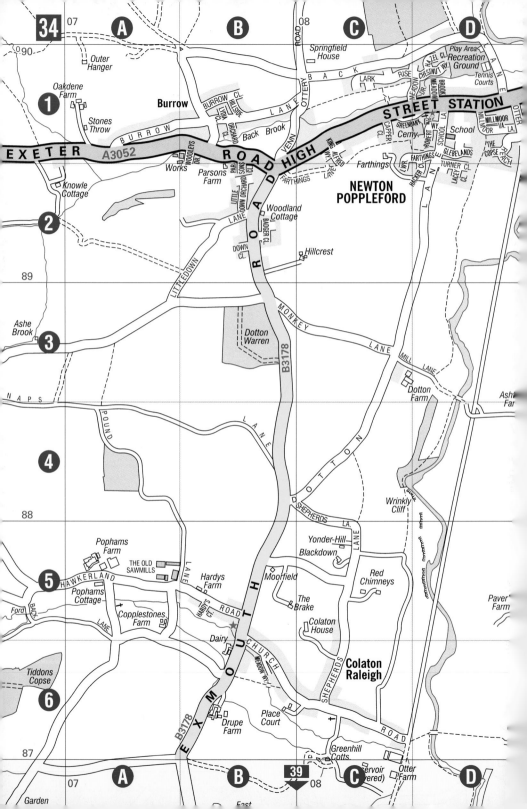

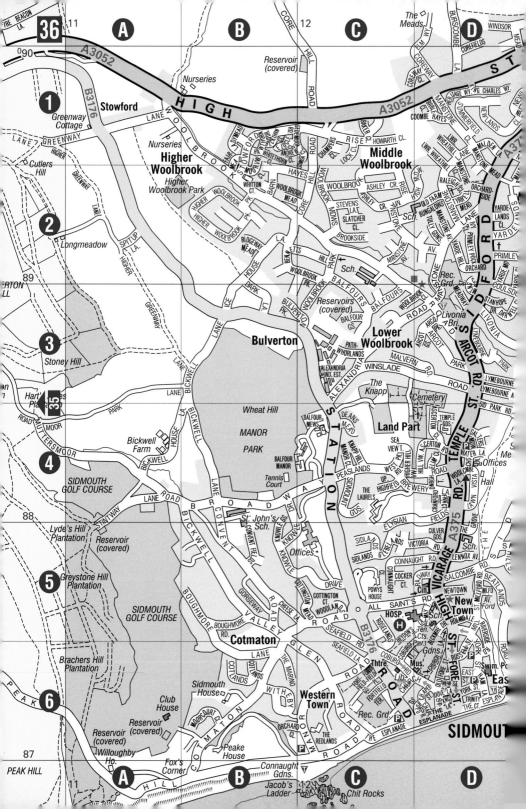

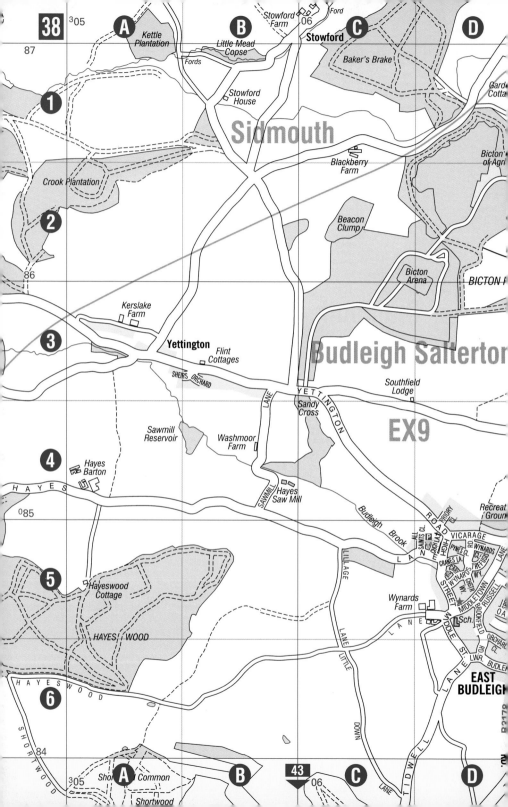

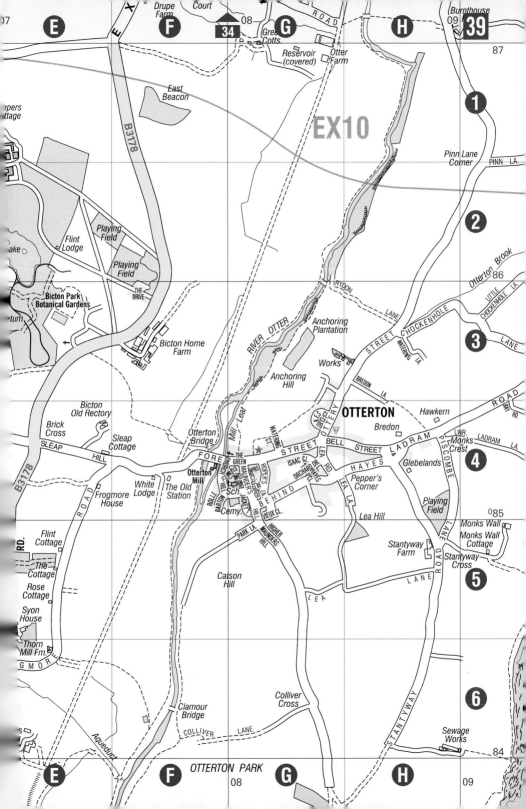

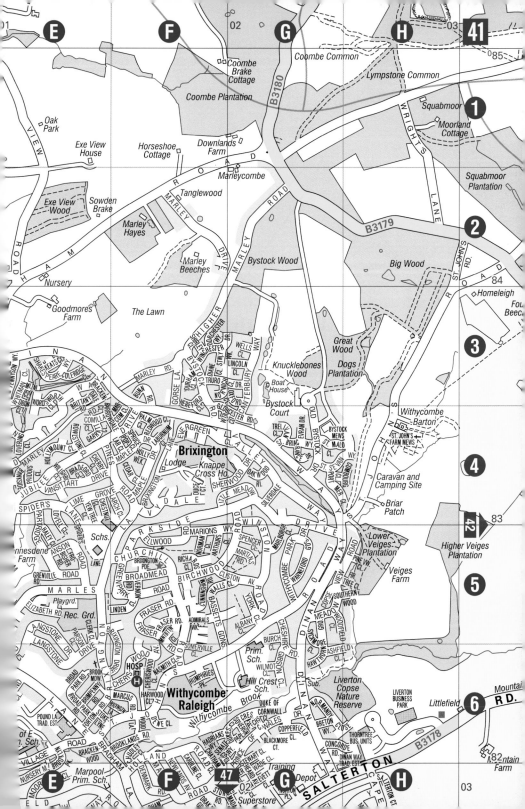

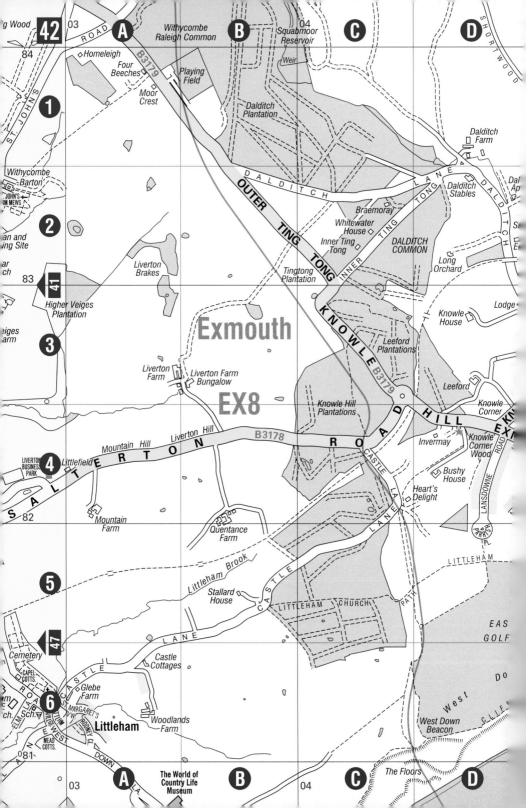

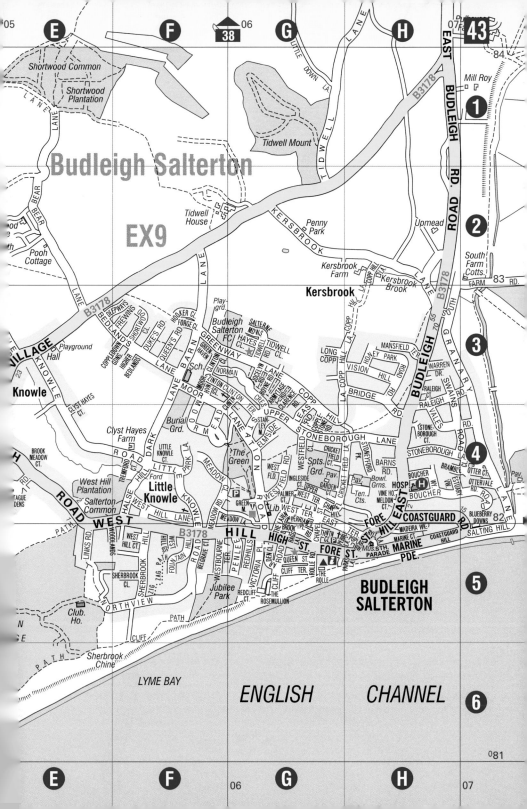

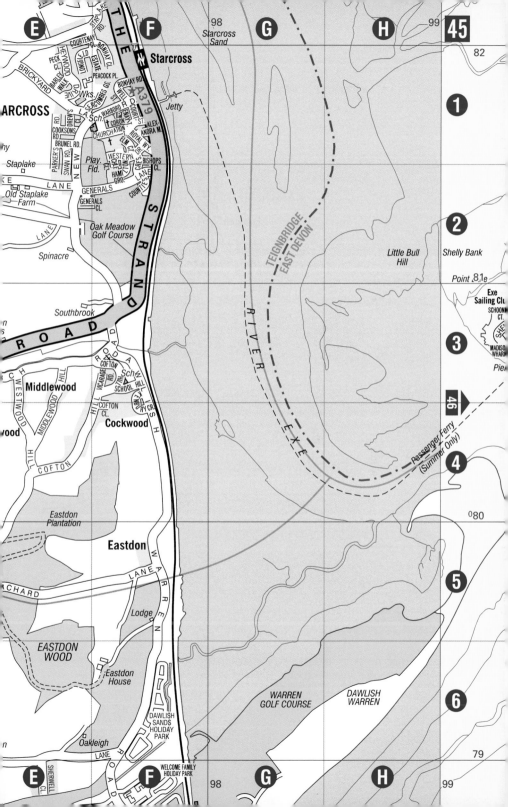

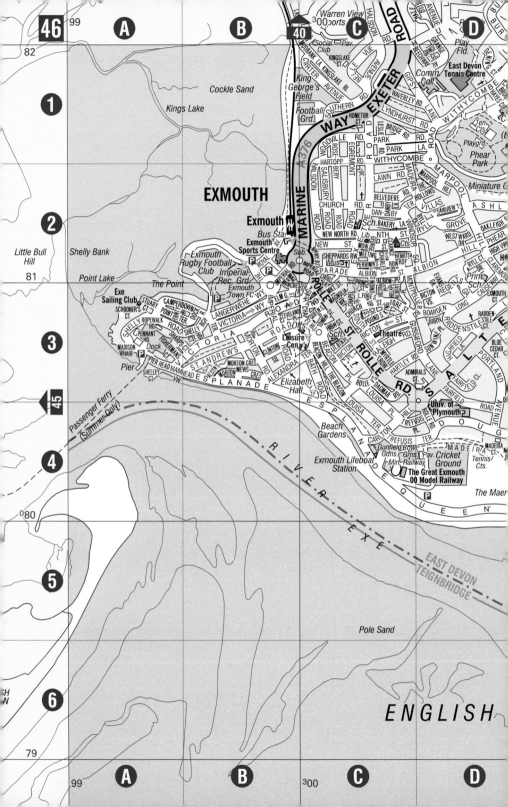

46 99 A B C D

82

1

Cockle Sand

Kings Lake

King George's Field

Warren View Sports

Social Club

Kingslake Ct.

Comm. Coll.

East Devon Tennis Centre

Play Fld.

Football Grd.

Phear Park

Miniature

EXMOUTH

2

Little Bull Hill

Shelly Bank

Point Lake

81

The Point

Exe Sailing Club

Exmouth Rugby Football Club

Exmouth Bus Sta.

Exmouth Sports Centre

Imperial Rec. Grd.

Exmouth Town FC

Withycombe

Church

Belvedere

Lib.

3

Schooner's Ct.

Shelly Ropewalk Rd.

Pennant Ho.

Madison Wharf

Pier

Shelley Ct.

Pier Head

Dock

Fisherman's

Camperdown

Point Ter.

St. Andrew's

Mamhead

Morton Mews

Morton Cres.

Langerwehe Wy.

Victoria

Leisure Cen.

Theatre

Rolle St.

45

Passenger Ferry (Summer Only)

Esplanade

Elizabeth Hall

Alexandra Ter.

Univ. of Plymouth

4

Beach Gardens

Exmouth Lifeboat Station

Gunfield Bowl Gdns.

Grnd. Pav. Min.-Railway

Cricket Ground

The Great Exmouth OO Model Railway

The Maer

80

R I V E R   E X E

Pole Sand

5

EAST DEVON TEIGNBRIDGE

6

79

E N G L I S H

99 A B C 300 C D

INDEX

Including Streets, Places & Areas, Hospitals & Hospices, Industrial Estates,
Selected Flats & Walkways, Stations and Selected Places of Interest.

HOW TO USE THIS INDEX

1. Each street name is followed by its Postcode District and then by its Locality abbreviation(s) and then by its map reference;
   e.g. **Abbey Rd.** EX4: Sto H. . . .4D **10** is in the EX4 Postcode District and the Stoke Hill Locality and is to be found in square 4D on page **10**.
   The page number is shown in bold type.

2. A strict alphabetical order is followed in which Av., Rd., St., etc. (though abbreviated) are read in full and as part of the street name;
   e.g. **Bennetts Hill** appears after **Bennett Cl.** but before **Bennett Sq.**

3. Streets and a selection of flats and walkways too small to be shown on the maps, appear in the index with the thoroughfare to which it is connected
   shown in brackets; e.g. **Adelaide Ct.** EX2: Exe. . . .6B **4** (off Queen's Rd.)

4. Addresses that are in more than one part are referred to as not continuous.

5. Places and areas are shown in the index in BLUE TYPE and the map reference is to the actual map square in which the town centre or area is located
   and not to the place name shown on the map; e.g. ALLERCOMBE. . . .3B **28**

6. An example of a selected place of interest is A-La-Ronde. . . .4C **40**

7. An example of a station is **Digby & Sowton Station (Rail).** . . .2A **18**

8. An example of a hospital or hospice is BUDLEIGH SALTERTON HOSPITAL. . . .4H **43**

GENERAL ABBREVIATIONS

All. : Alley	**Gdn.** : Garden	**Nth.** : North
Arc. : Arcade	**Gdns.** : Gardens	**Pde.** : Parade
Av. : Avenue	**Gth.** : Garth	**Pk.** : Park
Bri. : Bridge	**Ga.** : Gate	**Pas.** : Passage
Bldgs. : Buildings	**Gt.** : Great	**Pl.** : Place
Bungs. : Bungalows	**Grn.** : Green	**Ri.** : Rise
Bus. : Business	**Gro.** : Grove	**Rd.** : Road
Cvn. : Caravan	**Hgts.** : Heights	**Shop.** : Shopping
C'way. : Causeway	**Ho.** : House	**Sth.** : South
Cen. : Centre	**Ind.** : Industrial	**Sq.** : Square
Chu. : Church	**Info.** : Information	**St.** : Street
Cl. : Close	**La.** : Lane	**Ter.** : Terrace
Cnr. : Corner	**Lit.** : Little	**Trad.** : Trading
Cotts. : Cottages	**Lwr.** : Lower	**Up.** : Upper
Ct. : Court	**Mnr.** : Manor	**Va.** : Vale
Cres. : Crescent	**Mans.** : Mansions	**Vw.** : View
Cft. : Croft	**Mkt.** : Market	**Vs.** : Villas
Dr. : Drive	**Mdw.** : Meadow	**Vis.** : Visitors
E. : East	**Mdws.** : Meadows	**Wlk.** : Walk
Est. : Estate	**M.** : Mews	**W.** : West
Fld. : Field	**Mt.** : Mount	**Yd.** : Yard
Flds. : Fields	**Mus.** : Museum	

LOCALITY ABBREVIATIONS

Alp : **Alphington**	Ext : **Exton**	Sal R : **Salcombe Regis**
Broad : **Broadclyst**	Fen : **Feniton**	Shi S : **Shillingford St George**
Bud S : **Budleigh Salterton**	Hea : **Heavitree**	Sidm : **Sidmouth**
Cly H : **Clyst Honiton**	Hon : **Honiton**	Sow : **Sowton**
Cly G : **Clyst St George**	Ide : **Ide**	Star : **Starcross**
Cly M : **Clyst St Mary**	Kennf : **Kennford**	Sto H : **Stoke Hill**
Col R : **Colaton Raleigh**	Ken : **Kenton**	Top : **Topsham**
C Wear : **Countess Wear**	Lit : **Littleham**	W Hill : **West Hill**
Cow : **Cowley**	Lymp : **Lympstone**	Wheat : **Wheatley**
Daw W : **Dawlish Warren**	Nadd : **Nadderwater**	Whim : **Whimple**
E Bud : **East Budleigh**	New P : **Newton Poppleford**	Whip : **Whipton**
Ebf : **Ebford**	Ott : **Otterton**	Won : **Wonford**
Exe : **Exeter**	Ott M : **Ottery St Mary**	Wood : **Woodbury**
Exmin : **Exminster**	Penn : **Pennsylvania**	Wood S : **Woodbury Salterton**
Exm : **Exmouth**	Pin : **Pinhoe**	

A

	Adelaide Ct. EX2: Exe 6B **4**	**Albion Pl.** EX4: Exe 5B **10**
	(off Queen's Rd.)	EX8: Exm .2C **46**
	Admirals Ct. EX8: Exm 3C **46**	**Albion St.** EX4: Exe 1G **15** (5A **4**)
	Admirals Wlk. EX8: Exm 5F **41**	EX8: Exm .2C **46**
Abbeville Cl. EX2: Exe 3C **16**	**Alansway** EX11: Ott M 2C **30**	**Albion Ter.** EX8: Exm 2C **46**
Abbey Ct. EX2: Sow 1B **18**	A-La-Ronde 4C **40**	(off Henrietta Row)
Abbey Rd. EX4: Sto H 4D **10**	**Albany Cl.** EX8: Exm 5G **41**	**Aldborough Ct.** EX8: Exm 3E **47**
Abbots Rd. EX4: Sto H 4C **10**	**Alberta Cres.**	**Aldens Grn.** EX2: Alp 6H **15**
Aboveway EX6: Exmin 5B **22**	EX4: Sto H 3D **10**	**Aldens Rd.** EX2: Alp 6H **15**
Acland Pk. EX5: Fen 1H **27**	**Albert Pl.** EX8: Exm 3C **46**	**Alderson Dr.** EX2: Sow 1H **17**
Acland Rd. EX4: Exe 5B **10** (1F **5**)	**Albert St.** EX1: Exe 5B **10** (1G **5**)	**Aldrin Rd.** EX4: Sto H 2B **10**
EX5: Broad 4E **7**	**Albion Ct.** EX8: Exm 3C **46**	**Alexander Pl.**
Acland Ter. EX4: Exe 5A **10** (1F **5**)	(off Union St.)	EX11: Ott M 1D **30**
Addington Ct. EX4: Exe 5A **10**	**Albion Hill** EX8: Exm 2D **46**	**Alexandra M.** EX6: Star 1F **45**
Addison Cl. EX4: Exe 6E **9**		

Bird Cl. EX1: Pin 3A 12	Brickyard Rd. EX5: W Hill 3B 28	Bull Mdw. Rd. EX2: Exe 1A 16 (5E 5)
Birkett Cl. EX2: Won 2G 17	Bridespring Rd. EX4: Sto H 3D 10	BULVERTON 3B 36
Bishops Cl. EX6: Star 1F 45	Bridespring Wlk. EX4: Sto H 3D 10	Bulverton Pk. EX10: Sidm 3B 36
BISHOPS CLYST 3C 18	Bridford Rd. EX2: Alp 4A 16	Bunn Rd. EX8: Exm 3F 41
Bishops Ct. Ind. Est. EX2: Sow 2A 18	Bridge Cotts. EX4: Sto H 4B 10	Burch Cl. EX8: Exm 5G 41
Bishop's Ct. La. EX5: Cly M, Sow 3C 18	Bridge Ct. EX4: Exe 2B 4	Burgmanns Hill EX8: Lymp 2A 40
Bishop Westall Rd. EX2: C Wear 4E 17	BRIDGE END 1E 35	Burlands, The EX5: Fen 1H 27
Bittern Rd. EX2: Sow 6A 12	Bridgefield EX11: Ott M 1E 31	Burnet Cl. EX2: Won 3G 17
Blackall Rd. EX4: Exe 5A 10 (1D 4)	(off Chineway Rd.)	Burns Av. EX2: Won 3D 16
Blackboy Rd. EX4: Exe 5B 10 (1G 5)	Bridge Hill EX3: Top 3F 23	Burnside EX8: Exm 6D 40
Black Hat La. EX6: Wheat 3A 14	Bridgehill Gth. EX3: Top 3F 23	Burnthouse La. EX2: Won 3D 16
BLACKHORSE 4E 13	Bridge Rd. EX2: Alp, C Wear 6E 17	Burrator Dr. EX4: Exe 5E 9
Blackhorse La. EX1: Cly H 4C 12	EX6: Alp 1H 21	BURROW
Black Lion Ct. EX14: Hon 3E 33	EX8: Exm 1C 46	Broadclyst 3G 7
Blackmore Ct. EX8: Exm 6G 41	EX9: Bud S 3H 43	Newton Poppleford 1B 34
Blackmore Dr. EX10: Sidm 5D 36	Brimpenny Rd. EX8: Exm 6E 41	Burrow Cl. EX10: New P 1B 34
Blackmore M. EX2: Won 2G 17	Brittany Rd. EX8: Exm 3E 41	Burrow La. EX10: New P 1A 34
Blackmore Rd. EX5: Cly M 4H 19	Britten Dr. EX2: Won 1F 17	Burrow Rd. EX5: Broad 3F 7
Blackmore Theatre 3C 46	BRIXINGTON 4F 41	Burscombe La. EX10: Sidm 1D 36
Blackthorn Cl. EX10: Sidm 1B 36	Brixington Dr. EX8: Exm 5F 41	Buttery Cl. EX14: Hon 5E 33
EX14: Hon 5E 33	Brixington La. EX8: Exm 4F 41	Buttery Rd. EX14: Hon 5E 33
Blackthorn Cres. EX1: Hea 6G 11	(Brixington)	Butts Cl. EX14: Hon 6D 32
Blenheim Ct. EX2: Alp 5A 16	EX8: Exm 6E 41	Butts Hill EX6: Ken 1A 44
Blenheim Rd. EX2: Alp 4H 15	(Withycombe Raleigh)	EX11: Ott M 1E 31
Blueberry Downs EX9: Bud S 4H 43	Brixington Pde. EX8: Exm 5F 41	Butts Rd. EX2: Won 1E 17
Blue Cedar Ct. EX8: Exm 3D 46	BROADCLYST 3E 7	EX11: Ott M 1E 31
Bluecoat La. EX1: Exe 6A 10 (3D 4)	Broadclyst Sports Hall 5F 7	Byes Cl. EX10: Sidm 1E 37
Bluehayes La. EX5: Broad 1H 13	BROADCLYST STATION 1G 13	Byeside Rd. EX10: Sidm 1E 37
Boarden Barn EX8: Exm 3D 46	Broadfields Rd. EX2: Won 1G 17	Byes La. EX10: Sidm 1F 37
Bodley Cl. EX1: Hea 6F 11	Broadgate EX1: Exe 6H 9 (3C 4)	Byes, The EX10: Sidm 1E 37
Bodley Ho. EX1: Hea 5F 11	Broadleaf Cl. EX1: Pin 4A 12	(Fortescue)
Bogmoor La. EX5: Whim 2A 26	Broadmead EX5: Wood 5F 25	EX10: Sidm 5D 36
Bond's La. EX5: Wood, Wood S 4E 25	EX8: Exm 5F 41	(New Town)
Bonfire La. EX5: Wood 5F 25	Broadmeadow Av. EX4: Exe 2F 15	Byron Rd. EX2: Won 1G 17
Bonhay Cl. EX6: Star 1F 45	BROAD OAK 6F 29	Byron Way EX8: Exm 3E 41
Bonhay Rd. EX4: Exe 5G 9 (1A 4)	Broad Oak Cl. EX11: W Hill 6F 29	Bystock Cl. EX4: Exe 5H 9 (1B 4)
EX6: Star 1F 45	Broad Pk. Rd. EX8: Exm 6E 41	Bystock M. EX8: Exm 4G 41
Bonnington Gro. EX1: Hea 6D 10	Broadparks Av. EX4: Pin 2A 12	Bystock Rd. EX8: Exm 3F 41
Bonville Cl. EX1: Whip 5F 11	Broadparks Cl. EX4: Pin 2A 12	Bystock Ter. EX4: Exe 5H 9 (1B 4)
Booth Way EX8: Exm 5D 40	Broad St. EX11: Ott M 2D 30	
Border Rd. EX14: Hon 4C 32	Broadview EX5: Broad 4E 7	
Boucher Rd. EX9: Bud S 4H 43	Broadway EX2: Exe 3F 15	
Boucher Way EX9: Bud S 4H 43	EX5: Wood 6F 25	**C**
Boughmore La. EX10: Sidm 5B 36	EX10: Sidm 4B 36	
Boughmore Rd. EX10: Sidm 5B 36	Broadway Hill EX2: Exe 3E 15	Cadbury Gdns. EX9: E Bud 5D 38
Bourn Ri. EX4: Pin 2H 11	Broadway, The EX8: Lit 1G 47	Cadhay Cl. EX11: Ott M 2B 30
Bovemoor's La. EX2: Won 1D 16	Brodick Cl. EX4: Sto H 3B 10	Cadhay La. EX11: Ott M 1B 30
BOWD 1H 35	Brook Cl. EX1: Whip 4F 11	California Cl. EX4: Sto H 3B 10
Bowe Ct. EX1: Exe 1H 5	Brookdale EX11: Ott M 1E 31	Calm La. EX10: New P 3E 35
Bowhay La. EX4: Exe 1D 14	Brooke Av. EX2: Won 3D 16	Calthorpe Rd. EX4: Sto H 4D 10
(not continuous)	Brookfield Gdns. EX2: Alp 5H 15	Cambridge St. EX4: Exe 1G 15 (5A 4)
Bowling Green Marsh Nature Reserve 4G 23	Brookfield Rd. EX9: E Bud 5D 38	Cambridge Ter. EX4: Exe 1F 5
Bowling Grn. Rd. EX3: Top 4G 23	Brook Grn. Ter. EX4: Exe 5B 10	(off Oxford Rd.)
Bowring Cl. EX1: Hea 5F 11	Brookhayes Cl. EX8: Exm 1D 46	EX10: Sidm 5D 36
Boyne Rd. EX9: Bud S 3G 43	Brooklands Orchard EX11: Ott M 1E 31	(off Salcombe Rd.)
Bracken Cl. EX14: Hon 6B 32	Brooklands Rd. EX8: Exm 6F 41	Camelot Cl. EX4: Sto H 3E 11
Brackendale EX8: Exm 3E 41	Brookleigh Av. EX1: Hea 1F 17	Camilla Ct. EX4: Exe 1E 5
Brackendown EX11: W Hill 6F 29	Brooklyn Pk. EX8: Exm 6E 41	Camperdown Ter. EX8: Exm 3A 46
Brackenwood EX8: Exm 6E 41	Brook Mdw. EX8: Exm 6E 41	Campion Gdns. EX2: Won 3F 17
Bradfield Rd. EX4: Pin 3H 11	EX10: New P 1D 34	Campion Way EX14: Hon 6B 32
Bradford Cl. EX8: Exm 4E 41	Brook Mdw. Ct. EX9: Bud S 4E 43	Canaan Way EX11: Ott M 2D 30
Bradham Ct. EX8: Exm 1F 47	Brook Rd. EX9: Bud S 5G 43	Canal Banks EX2: Alp 3A 16
Bradham La. EX8: Exm 6E 41	Brookside EX10: Sidm 2C 36	Canberra Cl. EX4: Sto H 2C 10
Bradman Way EX2: Alp 4H 15	Brookside Cres. EX4: Sto H 2F 11	Candy's Path EX8: Lymp 2A 40
Bradninch Pl. EX4: Exe 2D 4	Brook St. EX11: Ott M 2D 30	Canon Way EX2: Alp 6H 15
Bramble Cl. EX9: Bud S 4H 43	Brookway EX1: Whip 5F 11	Canterbury Cl. EX5: Fen 1H 27
EX10: Sidm 1D 36	Broom Cl. EX2: Won 1E 17	Canterbury Rd. EX4: Exe 5E 9
Bramble Hill Ind. Est. EX14: Hon 3D 32	Brownlands Cl. EX10: Sidm 4E 37	Canterbury Way EX8: Exm 3G 41
Bramble La. EX14: Hon 4C 32	Brownlands Rd. EX10: Sidm 4E 37	Capel Cotts. EX8: Lit 2H 47
Bramley Av. EX1: Hea 6G 11	Brownlees EX6: Exmin 4A 22	Capel La. EX8: Lit 1H 47
Bramley Cl. EX6: Ken 1B 44	Browning Cl. EX2: Won 2E 17	Capper Cl. EX10: New P 1C 34
Bramley Gdns. EX5: Whim 5A 26	Brunel Cl. EX4: Exe 5G 9 (1A 4)	Carberry Av. EX8: Exm 6C 40
Bramleys, The EX14: Hon 1G 33	Brunel Rd. EX6: Star 1E 45	Carders Ct. EX2: Exe 1H 15 (5B 4)
Brand Cl. EX14: Hon 5E 33	Brunswick St. EX4: Exe 1G 15	Carlile Rd. EX2: Won 1E 17
Brand Rd. EX14: Hon 5E 33	Buchanan Cl. EX14: Hon 5D 32	Carlton Hill EX8: Exm 4C 46
Branscombe Cl. EX4: Exe 1E 15	Buckerell Av. EX2: Exe 3C 16	Carlton Rd. EX2: Won 2F 17
Branscombe La. EX5: Daw W 6A 44	Buckingham Cl. EX8: Exm 2G 47	Carlyon Cl. EX1: Hea 6E 11
Bredon La. EX9: Ott 3H 39	Buckingham Rd. EX2: Sow 3G 17	Carlyon Gdns. EX1: Hea 6E 11
Brent Cl. EX5: Wood 5G 25	Buckland Wlk. EX6: Exmin 3H 21	Caroline Cl. EX8: Exm 6F 41
Brenton Rd. EX6: Kennf 6C 20	Bucknill Cl. EX6: Exmin 4A 22	Carousel Ct. EX4: Exe 2G 15 (6A 4)
Brentor Cl. EX4: Exe 4F 9	Buddle La. EX4: Exe 1F 15	Carpenter Cl. EX4: Exe 6H 9 (4B 4)
Breton Way EX8: Exm 6G 41	Bude St. EX1: Exe 6A 10 (2E 5)	Carrington Pl. EX14: Hon 4F 33
Bretteville Cl. EX5: Wood 5G 25	Budlake Rd. EX2: Alp 5A 16	Carter Av. EX8: Exm 1C 46
Brewery La. EX10: Sidm 4C 36	Budleigh Hill EX9: E Bud 6D 38	Castle Farm EX11: W Hill 5G 31
Briar Av. EX2: Won 4D 16	BUDLEIGH SALTERTON 5G 43	Castle Ga. EX6: Ken 1B 44
Briar Cl. EX8: Exm 1F 47	BUDLEIGH SALTERTON HOSPITAL 4H 43	Castle Hill Vw. EX10: Sidm 1F 37
EX14: Hon 6E 33	Buller Cl. EX4: Exe 6A 4	Castle La. EX5: Wood 5G 25
Brickyard La. EX6: Star 1F 45	Buller Rd. EX4: Exe 1G 15 (5A 4)	EX8: Lit 2H 47
		EX9: Bud S 4C 42

Castle Mt.—Copse, The

Castle Mt. EX4: Exe 5H 9 (1C 4)
Castle St. EX4: Exe 6A 10 (2D 4)
Cat & Fiddle Pk. EX5: Cly M 3G 19
Cathedral Cl. EX1: Exe 6A 10 (3D 4)
Cathedral Yd. EX1: Exe 6A 10 (3C 4)
(not continuous)
Catherine St. EX1: Exe 6A 10 (3D 4)
Cauleston Cl. EX8: Exm 5C 40
Causey Gdns. EX1: Pin 3A 12
Causey La. EX1: Pin 3A 12
Cavendish Rd. EX1: Hea 6D 10
Cecil Rd. EX2: Exe 2G 15 (6A 4)
Cedar Cl. EX8: Exm 4F 41
EX14: Hon 4D 32
Cedars Rd. EX2: Exe 1A 16 (6E 5)
Cedars, The EX14: Hon 2G 33
Celia Cres. EX4: Sto H 2E 11
Cembra Cl. EX14: Hon 4F 33
Cemetery Pl. EX4: Exe 6H 9 (3B 4)
Central Av. EX2: C Wear 1D 22
EX4: Sto H 2F 11
Chamberlain Rd. EX2: Exe 2H 15 (6C 4)
Chambers Cl. EX10: Sidm 1C 36
Chancel Ct. EX4: Pin 3H 11
Chancel La. EX4: Pin 3H 11
Chancellor's Way EX4: Sto H 2E 11
Chandlers La. EX10: Sidm 4D 36
Chandlers Wlk. EX2: Exe 2H 15 (6C 4)
Chanter Ct. EX2: C Wear 4E 17
Chantry Mdw. EX2: Alp 6H 15
Chapel Ct. *EX2: Alp 5H 15*
(off Church Rd.)
Chapel Hill EX3: Cly G 2A 24
EX8: Exm 3C 46
EX9: Bud S 4G 43
Chapel La. EX11: Ott M 1E 31
Chapel Pl. EX3: Top 3F 23
Chapel Rd. EX2: Alp 5H 15
EX8: Lymp 2A 40
EX10: Sidm 6D 36
Chapel St. EX1: Exe 6A 10 (3D 4)
EX8: Exm 3C 46
EX9: Bud S 5G 43
EX10: Sidm 6D 36
EX14: Hon 3E 33
Chapple Cl. EX6: Star 2F 45
Chard Av. EX5: Whim 4A 26
Chard Rd. EX1: Hea 6E 11
Chardstock Cl. EX1: Whip 6H 11
Charingthay Ga. EX4: Sto H 4C 10
Charles Rd. EX14: Hon 3E 33
Charles St. EX8: Exm 2C 46
Charney Av. EX4: Exe 1E 15
Chase, The EX14: Hon 2F 33
Chatham Cl. EX8: Exm 6F 41
Chaucer Av. EX2: Won 3D 16
Chaucer Ri. EX8: Exm 3D 40
Cheeke St. EX1: Exe 6B 10 (2F 5)
Cheese La. EX10: Sidm 5B 36
Chelmsford Rd. EX4: Exe 6D 8
Cheltenham Cl. EX4: Exe 5E 9
Cheney's La. EX14: Hon 1G 33
Chepstow Cl. EX2: C Wear 6F 17
Cheriswood Av. EX8: Exm 6F 41
Cheriswood Cl. EX8: Exm 6F 41
Cherry Cl. EX8: Exm 4E 41
EX14: Hon 5B 32
Cherry Gdns. EX2: Won 2E 17
Cherry Tree Cl. EX4: Cow 1G 9
Cheshire Rd. EX8: Exm 5G 41
Chester Cl. EX4: Exe 5E 9
Chestnut Av. EX2: Won 3E 17
Chestnut Cl. EX8: Exm 4E 41
Chestnut Ct. EX2: Alp 6H 15
Chestnut Way EX10: New P 1D 34
EX14: Hon 5C 32
Cheynegate La. EX4: Pin 1G 11
Cheyne Ri. EX4: Pin 2H 11
Chichester Cl. EX8: Exm 2E 47
Chichester Ho. EX2: Won 1F 17
Chichester M. EX1: Exe 6A 10 (3E 5)
Chichester Way EX9: E Bud 5D 38
Chineway Gdns. EX11: Ott M 1F 31
Chineway Rd. EX11: Ott M 1E 31
Chiseldon Ho. *EX4: Penn 3G 9*
(off Copplestone Dr.)
Chiverstone Rd. EX6: Ken 1A 44
Chockenhole La. EX9: Ott 3H 39
Christow Rd. EX2: Alp 4H 15
Chudleigh Rd. EX2: Alp 6H 15
Chudley Cl. EX8: Exm 6F 41
Church Cl. EX5: Broad 3E 7
Church Hill EX4: Pin 1G 11
EX9: Ott 4F 39
EX14: Hon 4F 33
Churchill Cl. EX6: Ken 1A 44
Churchill Ct. EX8: Lymp 1A 40
Churchill Rd. EX2: Exe 2F 15
EX8: Exm 5F 41
Church La. EX2: Exe 2G 15 (6A 4)
EX2: Won 1D 16
EX4: Exe 5A 10 (1E 5)
EX4: Pin 2H 11
EX5: Broad 3E 7
EX5: Cly M 4D 18
EX9: E Bud 5D 38
EX10: Sidm 6D 36
Church Path EX2: Exe 6A 4
EX3: Top 3F 23
EX4: Exe 5G 9 (1A 4)
EX8: Lymp 2A 40
Chu. Path La. EX2: Won 1E 17
Chu. Path Rd. EX2: Exe 3F 15
Church Rd. EX2: Alp 4H 15
EX2: Exe 2G 15 (6A 4)
EX5: Whim 4A 26
EX6: Star 3E 45
EX8: Exm 2C 46
EX8: Lymp 2A 40
EX10: Col R 6B 34
Churchside EX5: Cly H 5F 13
Church Stile EX6: Exmin 4B 22
Church Stile La. EX5: Wood 5F 25
Church St. EX2: Won 1D 16
EX6: Ken 1A 44
EX6: Star 1F 45
EX8: Exm 3C 46
EX10: Sidm 1E 37
(Sidford)
EX10: Sidm 6C 36
(Sidmouth)
EX14: Hon 3E 33
Church Ter. EX2: Won 1D 16
Church Vw. EX11: Ott M 2D 30
Chute St. EX1: Exe 5B 10 (1G 5)
City Arc. *EX1: Exe 4C 4*
(off Smythen St.)
City Ind. Est. EX2: Exe 2A 16 (6D 4)
Clapperbrook La. EX2: Alp 5H 15
Clapper La. EX14: Hon 2E 33
Clapps La. EX11: Ott M 2D 30
Clara Pl. EX3: Top 3E 23
Claredale Rd. EX8: Exm 3D 46
Claremont Fld. EX11: Ott M 3D 30
Claremont Gro. EX2: Exe 2B 16 (6F 5)
EX8: Exm 2D 46
Claremont La. EX8: Exm 2E 47
Clarence Pl. EX4: Exe 5B 10
Clarence Rd. EX4: Exe 1G 15 (5A 4)
EX8: Exm 2C 46
EX9: Bud S 3G 43
Clarke Mead EX2: Won 2G 17
Claylands Vw. EX14: Hon 5D 32
Clay La. EX8: Lymp 3A 40
Clayton Rd. EX4: Exe 5G 9 (1A 4)
Clerk Cl. EX8: Exm 5E 41
Clevedon Cl. EX4: Sto H 3B 10
Clevedon Pk. EX10: Sidm 4E 37
Cleveland Ct. EX1: Exe 5B 10 (1G 5)
Cleveland Gdns. EX1: Exe 1G 5
Cleveland Pl. EX8: Exm 3B 46
Cleveland St. EX4: Exe 1G 15 (5A 4)
Cleve Rd. EX4: Exe 6F 9
Cliff Bastin Cl. EX2: Won 2G 17
Clifford Cl. EX1: Whip 5F 11
Clifford Rd. EX4: Sto H 4D 10
Cliff Path EX9: Bud S 6D 42
Cliff Rd. EX9: Bud S 5G 43
EX10: Sidm 6D 36
Cliff Ter. EX9: Bud S 5G 43
Clifton Hill EX1: Exe 5C 10 (1H 5)
Clifton Hill Sports Cen. & Ski Slope 5C 10 (2H 5)
Clifton Rd. EX1: Exe 6B 10 (2G 5)
Clifton St. EX1: Exe 6B 10 (2G 5)
Clinton Av. EX4: Sto H 4C 10
Clinton Cl. EX9: Bud S 3F 43
Clinton Sq. EX8: Exm 3B 46
Clinton St. EX4: Exe 1G 15 (5A 4)
Clinton Ter. EX9: Bud S 3G 43
Clipper Quay EX2: Exe 2A 16 (6D 4)
Cliston Av. EX8: Exm 5F 41
Cloister Rd. EX4: Sto H 5D 10
Cloisters EX1: Exe 6A 10 (4D 4)
Clover Av. EX4: Exe 4E 9
Cludens Cl. EX2: Alp 6H 15
Clydesdale Ct. EX4: Penn 3G 9
Clydesdale Ri. EX4: Penn 3G 9
Clydesdale Rd. EX4: Penn 3G 9
Clyst Ct. EX5: Cly M 3H 19
Clyst Halt Av. EX2: Sow 3A 18
Clyst Hayes Ct. EX9: Bud S 4E 43
Clyst Heath EX2: Sow 3H 17
CLYST HONITON 4F 13
Clyst Rd. EX3: Cly M, Top 1E 23
CLYST ST GEORGE 2A 24
CLYST ST MARY 3C 18
Clystside EX5: Cly H 4F 13
Clyst Valley Rd. EX5: Cly M 4D 18
Clysy Av. EX5: Broad 2G 13
Coastguard Hill EX9: Bud S 5H 43
Coastguard Rd. EX9: Bud S 4H 43
Coates Rd. EX2: Won 1F 17
Coburg Rd. EX10: Sidm 6C 36
Coburg Ter. EX10: Sidm 6C 36
COCKWOOD 3F 45
Codrington St. EX1: Exe 6B 10 (2G 5)
Coffins La. EX6: Exmin 5H 21
COFTON 4D 44
Cofton Cl. EX6: Star 4F 45
Cofton Hill EX6: Star 4E 45
Cofton La. EX6: Star 4D 44
Cofton Rd. EX2: Alp 5B 16
Colands Ct. EX2: Alp 6G 15
COLATON RALEIGH 6C 34
Coleridge Cl. EX8: Exm 3E 41
Coleridge Rd. EX2: Exe 2F 15
EX11: Ott M 1F 31
Colin Tooze Sports Cen. 2B 30
College Av. EX1: Exe 1B 16 (4G 5)
College La. EX2: Ide 4B 14
EX6: Ide 4B 14
College Rd. EX1: Exe 1B 16 (4G 5)
College, The EX2: Ide 4D 14
EX11: Ott M 1D 30
Colleton Cl. EX8: Exm 1E 47
Colleton Cres. EX2: Exe 1A 16 (5D 4)
Colleton Gro. EX2: Exe 2A 16 (6E 5)
Colleton Hill EX2: Exe 2A 16 (6D 4)
Colleton M. EX2: Exe 2A 16 (6E 5)
Colleton Row EX2: Exe 2A 16 (6E 5)
Colleton Way EX8: Exm 1E 47
Collins La. EX4: Sto H 2B 10
Collins Pk. EX9: E Bud 5D 38
Colliver La. EX9: Ott 6F 39
Colvin Cl. EX8: Exm 2F 47
Coly Rd. EX14: Hon 5E 33
Combourg Cl. EX8: Exm 4H 41
Comilla Cl. EX8: Exm 4E 41
Commercial Rd. EX2: Exe 1H 15 (5B 4)
Commin's Rd. EX1: Hea 5D 10
Compass Quay EX2: Exe 2A 16 (6D 4)
Concorde Rd. EX8: Exm 6G 41
Coney Ct. EX2: Exe 6C 4
Connaught Cl. EX10: Sidm 5C 36
Connaught Rd. EX10: Sidm 5C 36
Connections Discovery Cen. 6A 10 (2D 4)
Conrad Av. EX4: Whip 4F 11
Convent Flds. EX10: Sidm 5B 36
Convent Rd. EX10: Sidm 4B 36
Conway Ct. EX1: Exe 4F 5
Conybeare Cl. EX4: Whip 5F 11
Cooksons Rd. EX6: Star 1E 45
Coombe Cl. EX14: Hon 5E 33
Coombe Hayes EX10: Sidm 1D 36
Coombe St. EX1: Exe 1A 16 (4D 4)
Copperfield Cl. EX8: Exm 6G 41
Copp Hill La. EX9: Bud S 3G 43
Coppledown Gdns. EX9: Bud S 3E 43
Copplestone Dr. EX4: Penn 3G 9
Copplestone Rd. EX9: Bud S 4G 43
Copse EX8: Exm 5G 41
Copse, The EX2: C Wear 1C 22
EX10: New P 1D 34

Cordery Rd. EX2: Exe 3F 15
Corefields EX10: Sidm 1D 36
Core Hill Rd. EX10: Sidm 2C 36
(Higher Woolbrook)
EX10: Sidm 1D 36
(Middle Woolbrook)
Coreway EX10: Sidm 1D 36
Coreway Cl. EX10: Sidm 1C 36
Coriolis Way Nth. EX1: Whip ...5H 11
Coriolis Way Sth. EX1: Whip ...6H 11
Cornflower Hill EX4: Exe 4D 8
Cornhill EX11: Ott M 1D 30
Cornmill Cres. EX2: Alp 5G 15
Cornwall St. EX4: Exe 1G 15
Coronation Rd. EX2: Won 2E 17
Coronation Ter. EX6: Star 1F 45
Coronet Cl. EX2: Sow 3H 17
Cotfield Cl. EX14: Hon 2F 33
Cotfield St. EX2: Exe 3A 16
Cotlands EX10: Sidm 6B 36
COTMATON 5B 36
Cotmaton Rd. EX10: Sidm 6B 36
Cotterell Rd. EX5: Broad 2G 13
Cottey Cres. EX4: Sto H 2E 11
Cottington Ct. EX10: Sidm 5C 36
Cottington Mead EX10: Sidm ...5C 36
Cottles La. EX5: Wood 4G 25
Coulsdon Rd. EX10: Sidm 3D 36
Council La. EX5: Broad 6G 7
COUNTESS WEAR 6F 17
Countess Wear Rd. EX2: C Wear .5E 17
Counties Cres. EX6: Star 2F 45
County Ground 2G 15 (6A 4)
Couper Mdws. EX2: Sow 3H 17
Courtenay EX14: Hon 4C 32
Courtenay Cl. EX6: Star 1E 45
Courtenay Gdns. EX2: Alp 6G 15
Courtenay Rd. EX2: Alp 3H 15
Courtenay Ter. EX6: Star 1F 45
Courtfield Cl. EX11: W Hill 4F 29
Courtlands La. EX8: Exm 3B 40
Coventry Cl. EX5: Fen 1H 27
Coventry Rd. EX4: Exe 6F 9
Coverdale Rd. EX2: Alp 3H 15
Covetts EX5: Wood 5G 25
Cowick Hill EX2: Exe 3E 15
Cowick La. EX2: Exe 2F 15
Cowick Rd. EX2: Exe 2G 15 (6A 4)
Cowick St. EX4: Exe 2F 15 (6A 4)
COWLEY 1F 9
Cowley Bri. Rd. EX4: Cow, Exe ..1F 9
Cowper Av. EX2: Won 3C 16
Coysh Sq. EX3: Top 3E 23
Crabb La. EX2: Exe, Ide 4F 15
Craig Cotts. EX5: Cly M 3D 18
Cranbrook Rd. EX2: Won 1E 17
Cranes La. EX9: E Bud 5D 38
Cranford EX10: Sidm 4D 36
Cranford Av. EX8: Exm, Lit 3E 47
Cranford Cl. EX8: Exm 3E 47
Cranford Ct. EX8: Exm 3E 47
Cranford Ho. EX8: Exm 3F 47
Cranford Sports Club 3E 47
(off Salterton Rd.)
Cranford Vw. EX8: Exm 3E 47
Cranmere Ct. EX2: Alp 6B 16
Crawford Gdns. EX2: Exe 3G 15
Creadly La. EX3: Top 2F 23
Crealy Adventure Pk. 4H 19
Crediton Rd. EX5: Cow 1F 9
Creely Cl. EX2: Alp 6A 16
Crescent Mans. EX2: Exe 5F 5
Crescent, The EX8: Lit 1G 47
Cricketfield Ct. EX9: Bud S 4G 43
Cricket Fld. La. EX9: Bud S 4G 43
Cricklepit La. EX1: Exe 1H 15 (5C 4)
(off Cricklepit St.)
Cricklepit St. EX1: Exe 1H 15 (5C 4)
Critchards EX5: Wood 6G 25
Criterion Pl. EX8: Exm 3E 47
(off High St.)
Crockwells Cl. EX6: Exmin 5B 22
Crockwells Rd. EX6: Exmin 5B 22
Croft Chase EX4: Exe 2E 15
Cromwell Cl. EX1: Hea 1E 17
Cromwell Ter. EX2: Won 1H 17
(off Drake Av.)
Crosscut Way EX14: Hon 4E 33
Crossingfields Dr. EX8: Exm 6C 40

Cross La. EX10: Sidm 6D 36
(off Old Fore St.)
Crossmead Vs. EX2: Wheat 3D 14
Cross Vw. EX2: Alp 5H 15
Cross Vw. Ter. EX2: Ide 4E 15
Crowder's Hill EX8: Exm 4D 40
Crown Way EX2: Sow 3H 17
Crudges La. EX2: Exe 2C 46
Cuckoo Down La. EX14: Hon ...5G 33
Culverland Cl. EX4: Sto H 4B 10
Culverland Rd. EX4: Sto H 4B 10
Culvery Cl. EX5: Wood 5G 25
Cumberland Cl. EX8: Exm 6F 41
Cunningham Rd. EX8: Exm 5F 41
Curlew Way EX4: Penn 2A 10
Custance Ho. EX14: Hon 3E 33
(off Queen St.)
Cutteridge La. EX4: Wheat 1A 14
Cutters Wharf EX8: Exm 3A 46
(off Shelly Rd.)
Cygnet Ind. Units EX2: Sow 1A 18
Cypress Cl. EX14: Hon 6B 32
Cypress Dr. EX4: Exe 5F 9
Cyprus Rd. EX8: Exm 3D 46

D

Dagmar Rd. EX8: Exm 3C 46
Dairy Cl. EX6: Exmin 5B 22
Daisy Links EX4: Exe 4D 8
Dalditch La. EX9: Bud S 2B 42
Daleside Rd. EX4: Sto H 3C 10
Danby La. EX8: Exm 2C 46
Danby Rd. EX8: Exm 2C 46
Danby Ter. EX8: Exm 2C 46
Dane's Ct. EX4: Exe 5H 9
Dane's Rd. EX4: Exe 5H 9 (1D 4)
Danesway EX4: Pin 2A 12
Dark La. EX8: Exmin 6H 21
EX9: Bud S 4F 43
EX10: Sidm 3B 36
Darnell Cl. EX10: Sidm 3D 36
Dartington Wlk. EX6: Exmin 3H 21
Dart Wlk. EX2: Sow 2H 17
Darwin Cl. EX2: Exe 1A 16 (5E 5)
Dawlish Pk. Ter. EX8: Exm 3B 40
Dawlish Rd. EX2: Alp 1G 21
(Bad Homburg Way)
EX2: Alp 5H 15
(Clapperbrook La.)
EX6: Exmin 1G 21
Dawlish Sands Holiday Pk.
EX7: Daw W 6F 45
Dawlish Warren Rd. EX6: Star ..3F 45
EX7: Daw W, Star 3F 45
Days-Pottles La. EX6: Exmin 4E 21
EX6: Shi S 4E 21
Deacon Cl. EX2: Alp 6H 15
Deanery Pl. EX1: Exe 4D 4
Deans Mead EX10: Sidm 4C 36
Dean St. EX2: Exe 1A 16 (5E 5)
Deepdene Pk. EX2: Exe ...2C 16 (6H 5)
Deepway Ct. EX6: Exmin 4A 22
Deepway Gdns. EX6: Exmin 4H 21
Deepway La. EX2: Exmin 3F 21
EX2: Shi S 4F 21
EX6: Exmin 4G 21
Deepways EX9: Bud S 3E 43
De La Rue Way EX4: Pin 3H 11
Delderfield Gdns. EX8: Exm 3E 47
Delius Cres. EX2: Won 1G 17
Denbeigh Ter. EX10: Sidm 4D 36
Denbury Ct. EX2: Alp 6B 16
Dene Cl. EX8: Exm 6F 41
Dening Ct. EX8: Exm 1D 46
Denise Cl. EX2: Alp 6H 15
Denmark Rd. EX1: Exe 1B 16 (4F 5)
EX8: Exm 1F 47
Denver Cl. EX3: Top 2E 23
Denver Rd. EX3: Top 2E 23
Devon Ad. EX4: Sto H 4D 10
Devonshire Ct. EX14: Hon 5B 32
Devonshire Pl. EX4: Sto H 4B 10
Devonshire Regimental Mus. ...3C 16
Devonshire Rd. EX14: Hon 5A 32

Devonshire Way EX14: Hon 5C 32
Diamond Rd. EX2: Exe 2H 15 (6C 4)
Diane Cl. EX4: Exe 3F 41
Dickens Dr. EX2: Won 3D 16
Dick Pym Cl. EX2: Won 2G 17
Digby & Sowton Station (Rail) ..2A 18
Digby Dr. EX2: Sow 3H 17
Digby Ho. EX2: Sow 3H 17
Diggories La. EX14: Hon 3D 32
Dinan Way EX8: Exm 3E 41
Dinan Way Trad. Est. EX8: Exm .6H 41
Dince Hill Cl. EX5: Whim 4B 26
Dinham Cres. EX4: Exe 6H 9 (3A 4)
Dinham M. EX4: Exe 3B 4
Dinham Rd. EX4: Exe 6H 9 (3B 4)
Dix's Fld. EX1: Exe 6A 10 (3E 5)
Dock Rd. EX8: Exm 3B 46
Doctors Wlk. EX2: Ide 3D 14
(not continuous)
DOG VILLAGE 5F 7
Dorchester Way EX8: Exm 3F 41
Doriam Cl. EX4: Penn 2A 10
Dorset Av. EX4: Exe 2E 15
Dotton Cl. EX1: Whip 6H 11
Dotton La. EX10: New P 4C 34
Douglas Av. EX8: Exm 4D 46
Douglas Ct. EX8: Exm 3E 47
Dove Cl. EX14: Hon 5D 32
Dove La. EX10: Sidm 6D 36
Dove Way EX2: Wheat 3D 14
Dowell St. EX14: Hon 3D 14
Down Cl. EX10: New P 2B 34
Drake Av. EX2: Won 1H 17
Drake's Av. EX8: Exm 1F 47
EX10: Sidm 1E 37
Drakes Farm EX2: Ide 4E 15
Drakes Gdns. EX8: Exm 2G 15
Drakes Rd. EX4: Exe 2G 15 (6A 4)
Draycott Cl. EX2: Won 2E 17
Drew's Cl. EX2: Star 1E 45
Drive, The EX9: Col R 3F 39
Dryden Cl. EX8: Exm 3E 41
Dryden Rd. EX2: Won 2D 16
Dryfield EX6: Exmin 4B 22
Duchy Rd. EX14: Hon 5C 32
Ducks Orchard EX6: Exmin 5B 22
Duckworth Rd. EX2: Exe 2G 15
Duke of Cornwall Cl. EX8: Exm .6G 41
Dukes Cl. EX9: Ott 4G 39
Dukes Cres. EX8: Exm 6G 41
Duke's Rd. EX9: Bud S 3F 43
Dunchideock Rd. EX2: Ide 6D 14
Dunning Ct. EX14: Hon 3D 32
Dunrich Cl. EX2: Exe 1B 16 (4G 5)
Dunsford Cl. EX8: Exm 3F 47
Dunsford Gdns. EX4: Exe 3E 15
Dunsford Rd. EX2: Exe, Wheat ..3D 14
EX4: Exe 3D 14
Dunster Wlk. EX6: Exmin 3H 21
Dunvegan Cl. EX4: Penn 4G 9
Durbin Cl. EX14: Hon 4F 33
Durham Cl. EX1: Whip 5G 11
EX8: Exm 3F 41
Durham Way EX14: Hon 5C 32
DURYARD 2H 9
Dutch Ct. EX3: Top 4F 23
Dyers Ct. EX2: Exe 1H 15 (5B 4)

E

Eager Way EX6: Exmin 3H 21
Eagle Cotts. EX4: Exe 1G 15 (4A 4)
Eagles Nest EX2: Wheat 2D 14
Eagle Way EX2: Sow 1B 18
Eagle Yd. EX4: Exe 4B 4
Earl Richards Rd. Nth.
EX2: C Wear 3C 16
Earl Richards Rd. Sth.
EX2: C Wear 4D 16
East Av. EX1: Hea 5C 10
EAST BUDLEIGH 5D 38
E. Budleigh Rd. EX9: E Bud, Bud S .6D 38
(not continuous)
East Devon Tennis Cen. 1D 46
EASTDON 5F 45
East Dr. EX8: Exm 6C 40
Easter Hill La. EX6: Star 2D 44

I

Jacketts—Locksley Cl.

J

Jacketts EX9: Ott .4G **39**
James Ct. EX1: Exe .1A **16** (4D **4**)
James Owen Ct. EX4: Exe .1F **5**
Jarvis Cl. EX8: Lit .2G **47**
Jefford Ho. EX4: Penn .3G **9**
Jennifer Cl. EX2: Exe .3C **16**
Jerrard Cl. EX14: Hon .4E **33**
Jerrard Cres. EX14: Hon .4E **33**
Jesmond Rd. EX1: Exe .5C **10** (1H **5**)
Jesu St. EX11: Ott M .2D **30**
Jocelyn Rd. EX9: Bud S .3G **43**
John Hannam Ho. EX1: Exe .2F **5**
John Hudson Way EX8: Lit .2G **47**
John Levers Way EX4: Exe .1F **15**
John St. EX1: Exe .1H **15** (4C **4**)
Joslin Rd. EX14: Hon .5C **32**
Jubilee Cl. EX6: Exmin .4B **22**
Jubilee Ct. EX4: Exe .2C **4**
Jubilee Dr. EX8: Exm .4E **41**
Jubilee Gdns. EX10: Sidm .1E **37**
Jubilee Gro. EX8: Lymp .2B **40**
Jubilee Rd. EX1: Hea .5C **10**
Jubilee Sq. EX3: Top .4F **23**
Juniper Cl. EX4: Sto H .2F **11**
EX14: Hon .5C **32**
Jupes Cl. EX6: Exmin .5B **22**

K

Kalendarhay La. EX1: Exe .6H **9** (3C **4**)
Katherines La. EX11: Ott M .1E **31**
Kay Cl. EX8: Exm .1E **47**
Keats Cl. EX8: Exm .3E **41**
Keegan Cl. EX11: Ott M .2B **30**
Kenbury Cres. EX6: Star .3F **45**
Kenbury Dr. EX2: Alp .6A **16**
Kendall Cl. EX4: Exe .5B **10**
KENN .6B 20
Kennaway Rd. EX11: Ott M .1E **31**
Kennerley Av. EX4: Whip .4F **11**
KENNFORD .5B 20
Kennford Rd. EX2: Alp .3H **15**
Kenn La. EX6: Exmin .6H **21**
Kent Cl. EX2: Won .2E **17**
KENTON .1A 44
Kenton Hill EX6: Ken .1B **44**
Kenton M. *EX6: Ken .1A **44***
(off Fore St.)
Kenton Pl. EX2: Alp .4A **16**
KERSBROOK .3G 43
Kersbrook La. EX9: Bud S .2G **43**
Kerslake's Ct. EX14: Hon .3E **33**
Kerswill Rd. EX4: Exe .2F **15**
Kestell Rd. EX10: Sidm .5E **37**
Kestor Dr. EX4: Exe .4E **9**
Kestrel Way EX2: Sow .1A **18**
Keverel Rd. EX8: Exm .6C **40**
Kilbarran Ri. EX4: Penn .4G **9**
Kimberley Rd. EX2: Exe .1A **16** (5E **5**)
King Alfred Way EX10: New P .1C **34**
King Arthur's Rd. EX4: Sto H .2D **10**
King Charles Way EX10: Sidm .1D **36**
Kingdom M. EX4: Exe .5G **9** (1A **4**)
King Edward St. EX4: Exe .3G **9**
King Edward Studios
EX4: Exe .4E **9**
Kingfisher Av. EX2: Wheat .2D **14**
Kingfisher Dr. EX4: Penn .2B **10**
Kingfisher Way EX2: Sow .1A **18**
King Henrys Rd. EX2: C Wear .3C **16**
Kings Av. EX11: Ott M .1F **31**
Kingsgate EX4: Exe .4A **10**
Kingsgate Bus. Units *EX14: Hon .5C **32***
(off Devonshire Way)
Kingslake Ct. EX8: Exm .1C **46**
Kingslake Ri. EX8: Exm .1C **46**
Kings La. EX10: Sidm .6D **36**
Kingsley Av. EX4: Whip .4F **11**
Kings M. EX14: Hon .4D **32**
King's Rd. EX4: Sto H .4C **10**
EX14: Hon .3F **33**
King Stephen Cl. EX4: Exe .5A **10**
King's Ter. EX14: Hon .3E **33**
Kingston Rd. EX8: Exm .2E **47**
King St. EX1: Exe .1H **15** (4C **4**)
EX8: Exm .3C **46**
EX14: Hon .4D **32**
Kingsway EX2: Won .1D **16**
King's Wharf EX2: Exe .5D **4**
Kingswood Cl. EX4: Exe .4E **9**
King William St. EX4: Exe .6A **10** (1E **5**)
Kinnerton Ct. EX4: Exe .4F **9**
Kinnerton Way EX4: Exe .4D **8**
Kipling Dr. EX2: Won .2D **16**
Kitts La. EX10: New P .2E **35**
Knapphill EX10: Sidm .4C **36**
Knighthayes Wlk. EX6: Exmin .4H **21**
Knightley Rd. EX2: Exe .3C **16**
Knights Cres. EX2: Sow .3H **17**
Knightstone La. EX11: Ott M .4F **31**
Knightstone Rd. EX11: Ott M .4E **31**
KNOWLE .3E 43
Knowle Cl. EX14: Hon .3E **33**
Knowle Dr. EX4: Exe .5E **9**
EX10: Sidm .5B **36**
Knowle Gdns. EX10: Sidm .5B **36**
Knowle Hill EX9: Bud S .3C **42**
Knowle M. EX9: Bud S .2D **42**
Knowle Rd. EX9: Bud S .3E **43**
Knowle Village EX9: Bud S .4D **42**

L

Laburnum Cl. EX8: Exm .4F **41**
EX14: Hon .5B **32**
Laburnum Rd. EX2: Won .3D **16**
Lace Wlk. EX14: Hon .3E **33**
Lacey Cl. EX10: New P .2D **34**
Lackaborough Ct. EX2: Alp .6G **15**
Ladram Rd. EX9: Ott .4H **39**
Ladymead EX10: Sidm .1B **36**
Ladysmith Rd. EX1: Hea .5D **10**
Lake Cl. EX14: Hon .4F **33**
Lakelands Dr. EX4: Exe .6F **9**
Lakeside Av. EX2: C Wear .6F **17**
Lamacraft Dr. EX4: Whip .5E **11**
Lamb All. EX1: Exe .3D **4**
Lamplough Rd. EX8: Exm .4C **40**
Lancaster Cl. EX2: Won .1F **17**
Lancelot Rd. EX4: Sto H .2E **11**
Landhays Rd. EX4: Exe .1F **15**
LAND PART .4C 36
Landscore Rd. EX4: Exe .1F **15**
Lands Rd. EX4: Pin .3H **11**
Langaton Gdns. EX1: Pin .3B **12**
Langaton La. EX1: Cly H .3C **12**
EX1: Pin .3B **12**
LANGDON HOSPITAL .6C 44
Langerwehe Way EX8: Exm .3B **46**
Langford Av. EX14: Hon .3F **33**
Langford Rd. EX14: Hon .2F **33**
(Cheney's La.)
EX14: Hon .2F **33**
(Monkton Rd.)
Langstone Dr. EX8: Exm .5E **41**
Lansdowne EX2: Won .2F **17**
Lansdowne Rd. EX9: Bud S .4D **42**
Lansdowne Ter. EX2: Exe .1A **16** (5E **5**)
Larch Cl. EX8: Exm .4F **41**
Larch Rd. EX2: Exe .3F **15**
LARKBEARE
Exeter .2A 16 (6E 5)
Honiton .3G 27
Larkbeare Av. EX5: Whim .3G **27**
Larkbeare Rd. EX2: Exe .2A **16** (6E **5**)
Lark Cl. EX4: Penn .3B **10**
Lark Ri. EX10: New P .1C **34**
Laskeys La. EX10: Sidm .5E **37**
Latimer Rd. EX4: Sto H .4E **11**
Laurel Ri. EX8: Exm .1F **47**
Laurel Rd. EX2: Won .3D **16**
EX14: Hon .5B **32**
Laurels, The EX10: Sidm .4C **36**
Lavender Rd. EX4: Exe .4E **9**
Lawn Rd. EX8: Exm .2C **46**
Lawn, The EX9: Bud S .5G **43**
Lawn Vista EX10: Sidm .4D **36**
Lawrence Av. EX4: Exe .2G **15**
Lawrence Wlk.
EX6: Exmin .3H **21**
Laxton Av. EX1: Hea .6G **11**
Lea La. EX9: Ott .4G **39**
(not continuous)
Lea Rd. EX9: Ott .4G **39**
Leas Rd. EX9: Bud S .4G **43**
Lebanon Cl. EX4: Sto H .3C **10**
Lee Cl. EX14: Hon .3D **32**
Legion Way EX2: Alp .5H **15**
Leicester Mead EX4: Exe .5E **9**
Leigh Dene Cl. EX2: Exe .2C **16** (6H **5**)
Leighton Ter. EX4: Exe .5A **10** (1E **5**)
Le Locle Cl. EX10: Sidm .1B **36**
Lennox Av. EX10: Sidm .5D **36**
Leslie Rd. EX8: Exm .1C **46**
Lestock Cl. EX8: Lit .2G **47**
Lethbridge Rd. EX2: Won .1F **17**
Lewis Cres. EX2: Sow .3H **17**
Leypark Cl. EX1: Whip .5G **11**
Leypark Cres. EX1: Whip .6G **11**
Leypark Rd. EX1: Whip .5G **11**
Lichgate Rd. EX2: Alp .6H **15**
Liffey Ri. EX4: Exe .4E **9**
Lilac Rd. EX2: Won .3D **16**
Lillage La. EX9: E Bud .5C **38**
Lilley Wlk. EX14: Hon .4F **33**
Lily Mt. EX4: Exe .4D **8**
Lime Cl. EX5: Broad .4E **7**
Lime Gro. EX6: Exmin .3A **22**
EX8: Exm .4E **41**
Limegrove Rd. EX4: Exe .1F **15**
Lime Kiln La. EX2: C Wear .5E **17**
Limekiln La. EX8: Exm .4E **47**
Lime Tree Cl. EX2: Won .3G **17**
Lincoln Cl. EX5: Fen .1H **27**
EX8: Exm .3G **41**
Lincoln Rd. EX4: Exe .6E **9**
Linda Cl. EX1: Hea .1F **17**
Linden Cl. EX8: Exm .5F **41**
Linden Va. EX4: Exe .5H **9** (1B **4**)
Linfield Gdns. EX4: Exe .2F **15**
Linhay Cl. EX14: Hon .6D **32**
Links Cl. EX8: Exm .2E **47**
Links Rd. EX9: Bud S .5E **43**
Linnet Cl. EX4: Sto H .2B **10**
Lisa Cl. EX2: Won .2E **17**
Lister Cl. EX2: Exe .2C **16**
Litchfield Rd. EX4: Exe .6D **8**
Lit. Bicton Pl. EX8: Exm .3C **46**
Little Bri. Bus. Pk. EX5: Cly M .5F **19**
Lit. Castle St. EX4: Exe .6A **10** (2D **4**)
Lit. Chockenhole La. EX9: Ott .3H **39**
Little Cl. EX11: Ott M .2D **30**
Littledown Cl. EX8: Lit .2H **47**
Lit. Down La. EX9: E Bud .6C **38**
Littledown La. EX10: New P .3A **34**
Lit. Down Orchard EX10: New P .2B **34**
LITTLEHAM .2H 47
Littleham Chu. Path EX8: Lit .5B **42**
EX9: Bud S .5D **42**
Littleham Leisure Cen. .2H 47
Littleham Rd. EX8: Lit .2F **47**
Littleham Village EX8: Lit .2H **47**
Lit. John's Cross Hill EX2: Ide .3E **15**
LITTLE KNOWLE .4F 43
Lit. Knowle EX9: Bud S .4F **43**
Lit. Knowle Ct. EX9: Bud S .4F **43**
Littlemead La. EX8: Exm .4C **40**
Little Meadow EX8: Exm .4F **41**
Lit. Queen St. EX4: Exe .6A **10** (3D **4**)
Lit. Rack St. EX1: Exe .1H **15** (4C **4**)
Lit. Silver EX4: Exe .5H **9** (2B **4**)
Lit. Silver La. EX2: Shi S .3F **21**
LITTLETOWN .5D 32
Littletown Rd. EX14: Hon .5D **32**
Littleway EX2: Exe .3F **15**
Livermore Rd. EX14: Hon .4E **33**
Liverpool Hill EX4: Exe .5E **9**
Liverton Bus. Pk. EX8: Exm .6H **41**
Liverton Cl. EX8: Lit .1G **47**
Liverton Copse Nature Reserve .6G 41
Livery Dole Almshouses
EX2: Hea .1C **16**
Livonia Rd. EX10: Sidm .3D **36**
Lloyds Ct. EX1: Whip .4G **11**
Lloyds Cres. EX1: Whip .5G **11**
Locarno Rd. EX4: Exe .2F **15**
Lock Cl. EX10: Sidm .1C **36**
Lockfield Ct. EX2: Alp .5H **15**
Locksley Cl. EX2: C Wear .6E **17**

56 A-Z Exeter

Lockyer Av.—Mercer Ct.

Lockyer Av. EX10: Sidm 1E **37**
Lodge Hill EX4: Penn 4G **9**
Lodge Trad. Est. EX5: Broad 1G **13**
Longacres EX2: Exe 1B **16** (5G **5**)
Longbrook La. EX8: Lymp 3A **40**
Longbrook St. EX4: Exe 5A **10** (2E **5**)
Longbrook Ter. EX4: Exe 5A **10** (1D **4**)
Long C'way. EX8: Exm 3D **46**
Long Copp EX9: Bud S 3G **43**
Longdogs Cl. EX11: Ott M 2E **31**
Longdogs La. EX11: Ott M 2E **31**
Longdown Rd. EX6: Wheat 4A **14**
Longfield Est. EX6: Star 1E **45**
Long La. EX8: Exm 3E **47**
Longmeadow EX5: Cly M 3C **18**
EX5: Wood 5G **25**
Longmeadow Rd. EX8: Lymp 2B **40**
Long Pk. EX5: Wood 5G **25**
Lonsdale Rd. EX1: Hea 1E **17**
Looe Rd. EX4: Exe 5G **9** (1A **4**)
Loram Way EX2: Alp 6A **16**
Lords Way EX2: Won 3G **17**
Louisa Pl. EX8: Exm 3C **46**
Louisa Ter. EX8: Exm 4C **46**
Louvigny Cl. EX5: Fen 1H **27**
Lovelace Cres. EX8: Exm 1E **47**
Lovelace Gdns. EX2: Alp 6H **15**
Lovell Cl. EX8: Exm 4E **41**
Lovering Cl. EX8: Exm 4E **41**
Lwr. Albert St. EX1: Exe 6B **10** (2G **5**)
Lwr. Argyll Rd. EX4: Cow, Penn 3G **9**
Lower Av. EX1: Hea 6D **10**
Lwr. Brand La. EX14: Hon 5E **33**
Lwr. Broad Oak Rd. EX11: W Hill 6G **29**
Lwr. Budleigh EX9: E Bud 6D **38**
Lwr. Cloister Wlk. *EX6: Exmin* *3H* ***21***
(off Dunster Wlk.)
Lwr. Coombe St. EX1: Exe 1H **15** (5C **4**)
Lwr. Duck St. EX6: Exmin 5B **22**
Lwr. Farthings EX10: New P 2C **34**
Lwr. Fore St. EX8: Exm 3C **46**
Lwr. Griggs EX10: Sidm 2F **37**
Lwr. Halsdon La. EX8: Exm 6B **40**
Lwr. Harrington La. EX4: Pin 3A **12**
Lwr. Hill Barton Rd. EX1: Hea 6G **11**
Lwr. King's Av. EX4: Sto H 4B **10**
Lwr. Ladram La. EX9: Ott 4H **39**
Lower La. EX3: Ebf 4A **24**
Lwr. Marlpits Hill EX14: Hon 5F **33**
Lwr. Northcote Rd. EX14: Hon 2G **33**
Lwr. North St. EX4: Exe 6H **9** (2B **4**)
Lower Rd. EX5: Wood S 1E **25**
Lwr. St German's St. EX4: Exe 4A **10**
Lwr. Shapter St. EX3: Top 4F **23**
Lwr. Shillingford EX2: Shi S 2C **20**
Lwr. Summerlands EX1: Exe 6B **10** (2G **5**)
Lower Way EX10: New P 1E **35**
LOWER WEAR 1B 22
Lwr. Wear Rd. EX2: C Wear 6E **17**
Lwr. Wheathill EX10: Sidm 1D **36**
(not continuous)
LOWER WOOLBROOK 3C 36
Lucas Av. EX4: Exe 4B **10**
Luccombe La. *EX2: Exe* *3G* ***15***
(off Alphington Rd.)
Lucky La. EX2: Exe 1A **16** (5D **4**)
Ludwell La. EX2: Won 2E **17**
Lumley Cl. EX6: Ken 1B **44**
Lustleigh Cl. EX2: Alp 6A **16**
Lydia Cl. EX10: New P 1B **34**
Lymeborne Av. EX1: Hea 6E **11**
Lymebourne Av. EX10: Sidm 3D **36**
Lymebourne La. EX10: Sidm 3D **36**
Lymebourne Pk. EX10: Sidm 3D **36**
LYMPSTONE 2A 40
Lympstone Village Station (Rail) 2A 40
Lyncombe Cl. EX4: Sto H 3C **10**
Lyndhurst Rd. EX2: Exe 1C **16** (5H **5**)
EX8: Exm 1C **46**
Lynwood Av. EX4: Exe 1G **15** (4A **4**)

M

Macauley Cl. EX14: Hon 3G **33**
Madagascar Cl. EX8: Exm 1G **47**
Maddocks Row EX4: Exe 6H **9** (2C **4**)
Madeira Ct. EX8: Exm 4D **46**
Madeira Vs. EX8: Exm 2C **46**
Madeira Wlk. EX8: Exm 4D **46**
EX9: Bud S 5H **43**
Madison Av. EX1: Hea 6E **11**
Madison Wharf EX8: Exm 3A **46**
Maer Bay Ct. EX8: Exm 4D **46**
Maer La. EX8: Exm, Lit 4E **47**
Maer Rd. EX8: Exm 4E **47**
Maer Va. EX8: Exm 3E **47**
Magdalen Cotts. EX1: Exe 1B **16** (4F **5**)
Magdalen Gdns. EX2: Exe 1C **16** (4H **5**)
Magdalen Rd. EX2: Exe 1B **16** (4F **5**)
Magdalen St. EX2: Exe 1A **16** (4D **4**)
Magnolia Av. EX2: Won 3E **17**
EX8: Lit 1G **47**
Magnolia Cen. *EX8: Exm* *3C* ***46***
(off Chapel St.)
Magnolia Wlk. EX8: Exm 3C **46**
Magpie Cres. EX2: Wheat 2D **14**
Magpie La. EX14: Hon 6F **33**
Mahogany Cl. EX14: Hon 6C **32**
Main Rd. EX4: Pin 3A **12**
EX6: Exmin 2A **22**
(Dawlish Rd.)
EX6: Exmin 5C **22**
(Station Rd.)
Majorfield Rd. EX3: Top 3F **23**
Malden Cl. EX10: Sidm 2D **36**
Malden La. EX10: Sidm 1D **36**
Malden Rd. EX10: Sidm 1D **36**
Mallard Rd. EX2: Sow 1A **18**
Mallison Cl. EX4: Exe 4F **9**
Maltfield EX8: Lymp 2B **40**
Maltings, The EX2: Won 1D **16**
Malvern Gdns. EX2: Won 2E **17**
Malvern Rd. EX10: Sidm 3C **36**
Mamhead Rd. EX2: Won 2G **17**
EX6: Ken 2A **44**
Mamhead Vw. EX8: Exm 3A **46**
Manaton Cl. EX2: Alp 6A **16**
Manaton Ct. EX2: Alp 6A **16**
Manchester Rd. EX8: Exm 3B **46**
Manchester St. EX8: Exm 2B **46**
Mandrake Cl. EX2: Alp 5H **15**
Mandrake Rd. EX2: Alp 5G **15**
Manley Cl. EX5: Whim 4A **26**
Manna Ash Ct. EX2: Exe 6G **5**
Manor Cl. EX10: Sidm 4C **36**
EX14: Hon 4A **32**
Manor Cres. EX14: Hon 5E **33**
Manor Pk. EX5: Cly M 3C **18**
Manor Pavilion Theatre 6C 36
Manor Rd. EX4: Exe 1G **15**
EX10: Sidm 6C **36**
Mansfield Rd. EX4: Sto H 4C **10**
Mansfield Ter. EX9: Bud S 3H **43**
Manstone Av. EX10: Sidm 2D **36**
(Manstone La.)
EX10: Sidm 2C **36**
(Woolbrook Ri.)
Manstone Cl. EX10: Sidm 1D **36**
(High St., not continuous)
EX10: Sidm 2D **36**
(Manstone La.)
Manstone La. EX10: Sidm 3D **36**
Manstone Mead EX10: Sidm 1D **36**
Manston Rd. EX1: Hea 5C **10**
Manston Ter. EX2: Exe 1C **16**
Manstree Rd. EX2: Shi S 4A **20**
Manstree Ter. EX2: Shi S 4A **20**
Maple Cl. EX14: Hon 6B **32**
Maple Dr. EX8: Exm 4F **41**
Maple Rd. EX4: Exe 1F **15**
EX5: Broad 4F **7**
Marcom Cl. EX8: Exm 4F **41**
Marcus Rd. EX8: Exm 6F **41**
Margaret Rd. EX4: Sto H 3C **10**
Margaret St. *EX8: Exm* *3C* ***46***
(off Chapel St.)
Marina Ct. EX8: Exm 4D **46**
Marine Ct. EX9: Bud S 5H **43**
Marine Pde. EX9: Bud S 5H **43**
Marine Way EX8: Exm 2C **46**
Marino, The EX10: Sidm 6B **36**
Marions Way EX8: Exm 5F **41**
Maristow Av. EX8: Exm 5D **40**
Maritime Ct. EX2: Exe 2A **16** (6D **4**)
Marker Way EX14: Hon 5E **33**
Market Pl. *EX10: Sidm* *6D* ***36***
(off Church St.)
Market Sq. EX4: Exe 3C **4**
Market St. EX1: Exe 1H **15** (4C **4**)
EX8: Exm 3C **46**
Markham La. EX2: Alp 1C **20**
EX2: Shi S 6D **14**
Marlborough Cl. EX8: Exm 5G **41**
Marlborough Ct. EX2: Alp 6A **16**
Marlborough Dr. EX2: Won 1H **17**
Marlborough Rd. EX2: Exe 1B **16** (5G **5**)
Marles, The EX8: Exm 5E **41**
Marley Dr. EX8: Exm 2F **41**
Marley Rd. EX8: Exm 3F **41**
(Brixington)
EX8: Exm 5D **40**
(Hulham)
Marlpits La. EX14: Hon 4E **33**
Marpool Cres. EX8: Exm 1E **47**
Marpool Hill EX8: Exm 2D **46**
Marsh Barton Rd. EX2: Alp 3H **15**
Marsh Barton Trad. Est. EX2: Alp 4A **16**
Marsh Grn. Hill EX5: W Hill 5A **28**
Marsh Grn. La. EX5: W Hill 5B **28**
Marsh Grn. Rd. E. EX2: Alp 4A **16**
Marsh Grn. Rd. Nth. EX2: Alp 3A **16**
Marsh Grn. Rd. W. EX2: Alp 4H **15**
Marsh La. EX3: Cly G 2G **23**
Marshrow La. EX6: Exmin 6B **22**
Martins La. EX1: Exe 6A **10** (3D **4**)
Martins Rd. EX8: Exm 5G **41**
Marwood Pl. *EX14: Hon* *3F* ***33***
(off Langford Av.)
Mary Arches St. EX4: Exe 6H **9** (3B **4**)
Maryfield Av. EX4: Sto H 4B **10**
Marypole Rd. EX4: Sto H 3D **10**
Marypole Wlk. EX4: Sto H 3D **10**
Masefield Rd. EX4: Whip 4G **11**
Masey Rd. EX8: Exm 1F **47**
Matford Av. EX2: Exe 2B **16** (6G **5**)
Matford Bus. Pk. EX2: Alp 6B **16**
Matford Cen., The EX2: Alp 6B **16**
Matford La. EX2: Exe 2B **16** (6F **5**)
Matford M. EX2: Alp 1G **21**
Matford Pk. Rd. EX2: Alp 5A **16**
Matford Rd. EX2: Exe 2B **16** (6G **5**)
Mathews Cl. EX14: Hon 5D **32**
Matthews Ct. EX4: Pin 2H **11**
Maunder's Hill EX9: Ott 4G **39**
Maunders Pl. EX9: Ott 4G **39**
Mayfield Dr. EX8: Exm 3F **47**
Mayfield Rd. EX2: Won 1E **17**
EX4: Pin 3A **12**
Mayflower Av. EX4: Sto H 2B **10**
May St. EX4: Exe 5B **10**
May Ter. EX10: Sidm 5D **36**
Mead Cotts. EX8: Lit 2H **47**
Meadowbrook Cl. EX4: Exe 4E **9**
Meadow Cl. EX5: Cly M 3G **19**
EX8: Lymp 2B **40**
EX9: Bud S 4F **43**
EX11: Ott M 1E **31**
Meadow Dr. EX10: New P 1D **34**
Meadow La. EX9: Bud S 4G **43**
Meadow Rd. EX9: Bud S 5F **43**
Meadows Cres. EX14: Hon 4E **33**
Meadow St. EX8: Exm 2C **46**
Meadow Vw. Cl. EX10: Sidm 4E **37**
Meadow Vw. Rd. EX8: Exm 5G **41**
Meadow Way EX2: Won 1D **16**
EX10: Col R 6B **34**
Mead Vw. Rd. EX14: Hon 4E **33**
Meadway EX10: Sidm 3D **36**
Mecca Bingo
Exeter 3C 4
Mede, The EX3: Top 3E **23**
EX4: Whip 4F **11**
Medley Ct. EX4: Exe 4E **9**
Meeting La. EX8: Lymp 1A **40**
Meeting St. EX8: Exm 2C **46**
Meetways La. EX8: Exm 3F **47**
Melbourne Ct. *EX2: Exe* *5E* ***5***
(off Melbourne St.)
Melbourne Pl. EX2: Exe 1A **16** (5E **5**)
Melbourne St. EX2: Exe 2A **16** (6E **5**)
Meldon Ct. EX9: Bud S 4H **43**
Membury Cl. EX1: Whip 6H **11**
Mercer Ct. EX2: C Wear 4E **17**

A-Z Exeter 57

Oak Tree Pl.—Poltimore Sq.

Oak Tree Pl. EX2: Alp 6A 16
Oak Vw. EX14: Hon 5C 32
Oakwood Ri. EX8: Exm 4G 41
Oberon Rd. EX1: Whip 5A 12
Odeon Cinema
Exeter 1F 5
Odhams Wharf EX3: Ebf 3H 23
Oil Mill La. EX5: Cly M 4E 19
Oil Mill Rd. EX5: Cly M 4E 19
Okehampton Pl. EX4: Exe 1G 15 (5A 4)
Okehampton Rd. EX4: Exe 1F 15 (4A 4)
Okehampton St. EX4: Exe 1G 15 (5A 4)
Okewood Ct. EX8: Exm 3D 46
Old Abbey Ct. EX2: C Wear 3C 16
Old Bakery Cl. EX4: Exe 5F 9
Old Bystock Dr. EX8: Exm 3G 41
Old Coach Rd. EX5: Broad 4E 7
Old Dawlish Rd. EX6: Kennf 6D 20
Old Ebford La. EX3: Ebf 4A 24
Old Elm Rd. EX14: Hon 5B 32
Old Farm Bungs. EX10: Sidm 2D 36
Oldfields EX8: Exm 3E 47
Old Fore St. EX10: Sidm 6D 36
Old Ide Cl. EX2: Ide 4E 15
Old Ide La. EX2: Ide 4E 15
Old Mkt. Cl. EX2: Alp 3H 15
Old Matford La. EX2: Alp, Exmin 1F 21
Old Mill Cl. EX2: Exe 2B 16 (6E 5)
Old Okehampton Rd. EX4: Nadd 5A 8
Oldpark Rd. EX4: Exe 5A 10 (1E 5)
Old Pavilion Cl. EX2: Won 2G 17
Old Pinn La. EX1: Pin 3A 12
Old Rydon Cl. EX2: C Wear 4A 18
Old Rydon La. EX2: C Wear 5G 17
Old Rydon Ley EX2: C Wear 4H 17
Old Sawmills, The EX10: Col R 5A 34
Old's Vw. EX4: Exe 5G 9
Old Tiverton Rd. EX4: Exe, Sto H 5B 10 (1G 5)
Old Vicarage Cl. EX2: Ide 5D 14
Old Vicarage Rd. EX2: Exe 2G 15
Olga Ter. EX8: Lymp 2B 40
Orchard Cl. EX1: Pin 3B 12
EX5: Wood 5G 25
EX8: Exm 6D 40
EX8: Lymp 2A 40
EX9: E Bud 5D 38
EX10: New P 1B 34
EX10: Sidm 1E 37
(Sidford)
EX10: Sidm 6B 36
(Western Town)
EX11: Ott M 2E 31
Orchard Ct. EX5: Whim 4A 26
Orchard Dr. EX9: Ott 4G 39
Orchard Gdns. EX4: Exe 2F 15
EX5: Broad 4F 7
Orchard Hill EX2: Exe 3E 15
Orchard La. EX6: Star 5E 45
Orchardside EX10: Sidm 2D 36
Orchard, The EX14: Hon 4D 32
(Honiton)
EX14: Hon 2H 33
(Northcote)
Orchard Vw. EX1: Hea 1D 16
Orchard Way EX3: Top 3E 23
EX6: Ken 1A 44
EX14: Hon 3F 33
(not continuous)
Orcombe Ct. EX8: Lit 1F 47
Oriole Dr. EX4: Penn 3B 10
Orwell Gth. EX4: Whip 4G 11
Osprey Rd. EX2: Sow 6B 12
Otago Cotts. EX2: Exe 3C 16
Otterbourne Ct. EX9: Bud S 5H 43
(off Coastguard Rd.)
Otter Cl. EX11: W Hill 5F 29
Otter Ct. EX2: Alp 6A 16
EX9: Bud S 4H 43
Otter Reach EX10: New P 1D 34
OTTERTON 4G 39
Otterton Mill 4F 39
Ottervale Rd. EX9: Bud S 4H 43
Otter Valley Pk. EX14: Hon 1H 33
Ottery Moor EX14: Hon 3D 32
Ottery Moor La. EX14: Hon 3C 32
Ottery Rd. EX5: Fen 1H 27
OTTERY ST MARY 2D 30
OTTERY ST MARY HOSPITAL 2B 30
Ottery St. EX9: Ott 4G 39
Outer Ting Tong EX9: Bud S 2B 42
Oval Grn. EX2: Won 3G 17
(off Old Pavilion Cl.)
Oxford Cl. EX8: Exm 3G 41
Oxford Rd. EX4: Exe 5B 10 (1F 5)
Oxford St. EX2: Exe 2G 15 (6A 4)

P

Packhorse Cl. EX10: Sidm 1F 37
Painters Ct. EX2: Exe 2H 15 (6C 4)
Palace Cotts. EX8: Exm 2C 46
(off Parade)
Palace Ga. EX1: Exe 1A 16 (3D 4)
Pale Ga. Cl. EX14: Hon 2F 33
Palm Cl. EX8: Exm 4F 41
Palmer Ct. EX9: Bud S 4G 43
Palmer's La. EX5: W Hill 4B 28
Palmerston Dr. EX4: Exe 5E 9
Pamela Rd. EX1: Hea 5D 10
Pancras Sq. EX4: Exe 3C 4
Pankhurst Cl. EX8: Lit 2G 47
Panney, The EX4: Whip 5E 11
Parade EX8: Exm 2C 46
Paris St. EX1: Exe 6A 10 (2E 5)
Paris St. Arc. EX1: Exe 2E 5
Park & Ride
Digby for Royal Devon & Exeter Hospital (Wonford) 2H 17
Honiton Road 6A 12
Matford 1F 21
Sowton 2A 18
Park Cl. EX5: Wood 6G 25
Parkers Cross La. EX1: Pin 2B 12
Parker's Rd. EX6: Star 2E 45
Parkfield Rd. EX3: Top 3F 23
Parkfield Way EX3: Top 3F 23
Park Five Bus. Cen. EX2: Sow 2A 18
Parkhayes EX5: Wood S 1G 25
Parkhouse Rd. EX2: Exe 3F 15
Parkland Dr. EX2: Won 3G 17
Park La. EX4: Pin 1H 11
EX8: Exm 1C 46
EX9: Bud S 4F 43
EX9: Ott 5G 39
Park Pl. EX1: Hea 6D 10
EX2: Exe 1B 16 (5G 5)
Park Rd. EX1: Hea 5C 10 (1H 5)
EX8: Exm 1C 46
Parkside Cres. EX1: Pin 1B 12
Parkside Dr. EX8: Exm 5F 41
Parkside Rd. EX1: Pin 1B 12
Parks La. EX9: Bud S 5H 43
Park Way EX5: Wood 6G 25
EX8: Exm 1E 47
(not continuous)
Parkway EX2: Exe 3F 15
Parliament St. EX4: Exe 6H 9 (3C 4)
Parr Cl. EX1: Exe 5B 10 (1G 5)
Parr St. EX1: Exe 5B 10 (1G 5)
Parsonage La. EX14: Hon 4F 33
Parsonage Way EX5: Wood 5G 25
Parson Cl. EX8: Exm 5E 41
Parsons Cl. EX10: New P 2B 34
Parthia Pl. EX8: Exm 6G 41
Partridge Rd. EX8: Exm 4E 41
Passaford La. EX10: New P, Sidm 5E 35
Paternoster Row EX11: Ott M 1D 30
Pathwhorlands EX10: Sidm 3C 36
Patricia Cl. EX4: Penn 2A 10
Patteson Dr. EX11: Ott M 1F 31
Paul St. EX4: Exe 6H 9 (3C 4)
Pavilion Pl. EX2: Exe 1A 16 (4E 5)
Paynes Ct. EX4: Whip 4F 11
Peacock Pl. EX6: Star 1F 45
Peak Hill Rd. EX10: Sidm 6G 35
Pear Tree Cl. EX6: Ken 1B 44
Peaslands Rd. EX10: Sidm 4C 36
Pebble La. EX9: Bud S 5G 43
Peep La. EX4: Exe 6G 9 (2A 4)
Pegasus Ct. EX1: Hea 6D 10
Pellinore Rd. EX4: Sto H 3E 11
Pendle EX9: Bud S 5G 43
Pendragon Rd. EX4: Sto H 2D 10
Penhayes Cl. EX6: Ken 1B 44
Penhayes Rd. EX6: Ken 1B 44
Peninsula Pk. EX2: Won 2G 17
Penitentiary Ct. EX2: Exe 1A 16 (5D 4)
Penleonard Cl. EX2: Exe 1C 16 (5H 5)
Pennant Ho. EX8: Exm 3A 46
PENNSYLVANIA 3B 10
Pennsylvania Cl. EX4: Sto H 4B 10
Pennsylvania Ct. EX4: Penn 4B 10
Pennsylvania Cres. EX4: Exe 4A 10
Pennsylvania Pk. EX4: Sto H 3B 10
Pennsylvania Rd. EX4: Cow, Penn 1A 10
EX4: Exe, Sto H 5A 10
Penny Cl. EX6: Exmin 4A 22
Pentgrove Ct. EX8: Exm 2F 47
Perceval Rd. EX4: Sto H 3E 11
Percy Rd. EX2: Alp 3H 15
Perriam's Pl. EX9: Bud S 4G 43
Perridge Cl. EX2: Wheat 3E 15
Perriman's Row EX8: Exm 2C 46
Perry Rd. EX4: Penn 4H 9
Perrys Gdns. EX11: W Hill 5F 29
Perth Cl. EX4: Sto H 2C 10
Peryam Cres. EX2: Won 2E 17
Peterborough Rd. EX4: Exe 5E 9
Phear Av. EX8: Exm 2D 46
Philip Rd. EX4: Sto H 4D 10
Phillipps Av. EX8: Exm 6D 40
Phillips Sq. EX14: Hon 3D 32
Piccadilly La. EX11: Ott M 2D 30
(off Hind St.)
Pickwick Arc. EX4: Exe 4C 4
Pier Head EX8: Exm 3A 46
Pilgrim Ho. EX4: Sto H 4D 10
Pilot Wharf EX8: Exm 3A 46
(off Victoria Rd.)
Pilton La. EX1: Pin 4H 11
Pinaster Cl. EX14: Hon 4G 33
Pinbridge M. EX4: Pin 3H 11
Pinbrook M. EX4: Sto H 2G 11
Pinbrook Rd. EX4: Pin 3H 11
Pinces Cotts. EX2: Exe 3G 15
Pinces Gdns. EX2: Exe 3G 15
Pinces Rd. EX2: Exe 3G 15
Pine Av. EX4: Exe 5F 9
Pinefields Cl. EX11: W Hill 6G 29
Pine Gdns. EX14: Hon 3F 33
Pine Gro. EX14: Hon 3F 33
Pine Pk. Rd. EX14: Hon 4F 33
Pineridge Cl. EX4: Exe 2F 15
Pines Rd. EX8: Exm 4E 41
Pines, The EX4: Exe 5F 9
EX14: Hon 4F 33
Pine Vw. Cl. EX8: Exm 5H 41
PINHOE 2A 12
Pinhoe Rd. EX4: Hea 5C 10
Pinhoe Station (Rail) 3A 12
Pinhoe Trad. Est. EX4: Pin 3H 11
(not continuous)
Pinncourt La. EX1: Pin 2B 12
Pinn Hill EX1: Pin 2B 12
Pinn La. EX1: Pin, Whip 3A 12
EX10: Ott 2H 39
Pinn Valley Rd. EX1: Pin 3B 12
Pinwood La. EX4: Sto H 2F 11
(not continuous)
Pinwood Mdw. Dr. EX4: Sto H 2F 11
Pippin Cl. EX1: Hea 6G 11
Piscombe La. EX9: Ott 4H 39
Pitson La. EX10: New P 4E 35
Pitt Hill EX6: Ken 1A 44
Pitts Ct. EX2: Exe 2B 16
(off Weirside Pl.)
Plantaganet Wlk. EX2: Sow 2H 17
Plassey Cl. EX4: Sto H 2B 10
Playmoor Dr. EX1: Pin 3B 12
Plume of Feathers Cl.
EX11: Ott M 1E 31
Plumtree Dr. EX2: Won 2F 17
Plumtree La. EX5: Whim 6B 26
Point Ter. EX8: Exm 3A 46
Polehouse La. EX2: Ide 6E 15
POLSLOE BRIDGE 5E 11
Polsloe Bridge Station (Rail) 5E 11
POLSLOE PARK 5C 10 (1H 5)
POLSLOE PRIORY 4D 10
Polsloe Rd. EX1: Exe, Hea 5C 10 (1H 5)
POLTIMORE 4B 6
Poltimore Ct. EX4: Broad 3B 6
Poltimore Sq. EX4: Exe 5A 10 (1E 5)

A-Z Exeter 59

Poplar Cl.—Rowhorne Rd.

Poplar Cl. EX2: Exe 3G **15**
EX8: Exm 4F **41**
Poplar Row EX9: Bud S 5H **43**
Poplars, The EX4: Pin 2A **12**
Poplars Wlk. *EX5: Cly M* *4F* ***19***
(off Hazelmead Rd.)
Poppy Cl. EX4: Exe 4D **8**
Porchester Hgts. *EX4: Exe* *1F* ***5***
(off Acland Rd.)
Portland Av. EX8: Exm 3D **46**
Portland St. EX1: Exe 6C **10** (1G **5**)
Portmer Cl. EX8: Exm 4G **41**
Port Rd. EX7: Daw W 5A **44**
Post Office St. EX1: Exe 6A **10** (3E **5**)
Potters Cl. EX11: W Hill 4F **29**
Pottery Cl. EX14: Hon 3F **33**
Pottles Cl. EX6: Exmin 5A **22**
Pound Cl. EX3: Top 2E **23**
EX8: Exm 6E **41**
Pound La. EX3: Top 2E **23**
EX5: Wood 5G **25**
EX8: Exm 5D **40**
EX10: Col R 4A **34**
Pound La. Trad. Est. EX8: Exm 6E **41**
Poundsland EX5: Broad 4E **7**
Pound St. EX8: Exm 3C **46**
Powderham Castle 1C 44
Powderham Cl. EX3: Top 2E **23**
Powderham Cres. EX4: Sto H 4B **10**
Powderham Rd. EX2: Exe 2G **15**
Powderham Wlk. EX6: Exmin 3H **21**
Powhay Mills EX4: Exe 1H **15** (4A **4**)
Powlesland Rd. EX2: Alp 5H **15**
Powys Ho. EX10: Sidm 5C **36**
Premier Pl. EX2: Exe 1B **16** (5G **5**)
Prescot Rd. EX4: Exe 1E **15**
Preston St. EX1: Exe 1H **15** (4C **4**)
Pretoria Rd. EX1: Hea 5D **10**
Priddis Cl. EX8: Exm 4E **41**
Pridhams Way EX6: Exmin 4A **22**
Priestley Av. EX4: Whip 4F **11**
Primley Gdns. EX10: Sidm 2E **37**
Primley Mead EX10: Sidm 2E **37**
Primley Paddock EX10: Sidm 2D **36**
Primley Rd. EX10: Sidm 2E **37**
(Primley Mead)
Primley Rd. EX10: Sidm 2D **36**
(Sidford Rd.)
Primrose Lawn EX4: Exe 4D **8**
Prince Charles Cl. EX8: Exm 6G **41**
Prince Charles Rd. EX4: Sto H 4C **10**
Prince of Wales Dr. EX8: Exm 1F **47**
Prince of Wales Rd. EX4: Penn 4H **9**
Princesshay EX1: Exe 6A **10** (3D **4**)
Prince's Sq. EX2: Exe 2G **15**
Princes St. EX8: Exm 3C **46**
Prince's St. E. EX2: Exe 3G **15**
Prince's St. Nth. EX2: Exe 2G **15**
Prince's St. Sth. EX2: Exe 3G **15**
Prince's St. W. EX2: Exe 2G **15**
Priory Cl. EX9: E Bud 4D **38**
Priory Rd. EX4: Sto H 4C **10**
Prison La. EX4: Exe 5A **10** (1D **4**)
Prospect Gdns. EX4: Exe 5C **10**
Prospect Pk. EX4: Sto H 4B **10**
Prospect Pl. EX4: Exe 2G **15**
EX11: Ott M 2D **30**
Puckridge Rd. EX4: Pin 2H **11**
Puffin Way EX2: Wheat 3D **14**
Pulling Rd. EX4: Pin 2H **11**
Pulpit Wlk. EX2: Alp 1E **21**
Purcell Cl. EX2: Won 1G **17**
Pye Cnr. EX6: Kennf 6D **20**
Pynes Cl. EX9: E Bud 5D **38**
Pynes Hill EX2: C Wear 4F **17**
Pynes Hill Bus. Pk. EX2: C Wear 4G **17**
Pyramids Swimming & Leisure Cen., The 6B 10 (3F 5)
Pytte Gdns. EX3: Cly G 1A **24**

Q

Quadrangle, The EX4: Exe 5A **10**
Quadrant, The EX2: Exe 1B **16** (5F **5**)
Quarries, The EX4: Exe 2D **14**
Quarry La. EX2: Sow, Won 1F **17**
Quarry Pk. Rd. EX2: Won 2G **17**
Quarter Mile La. EX5: W Hill 6A **28**
Quay Hill EX2: Exe 1H **15** (5C **4**)
Quay House Vis. Cen. 1H 15 (5D 4)
Quay La. EX2: Exe 1A **16** (5D **4**)
EX8: Lymp 3A **40**
Quay Steps EX2: Exe 5D **4**
Quay, The EX2: Exe 1A **16** (5D **4**)
Queen's Ct. *EX8: Exm* *3C* ***46***
(off Queen St.)
Queen's Cres. EX4: Exe 5A **10** (1E **5**)
Queen's Dr. EX8: Exm 4D **46**
Queens Dr., The EX4: Penn 4H **9**
Queensland Dr. EX4: Sto H 2C **10**
Queen's Rd. EX2: Exe 3G **15** (6B **4**)
EX9: Bud S 3F **43**
Queen's Ter. EX4: Exe 5H **9** (1B **4**)
Queen St. EX4: Exe 5H **9** (1C **4**)
EX8: Exm 3C **46**
EX9: Bud S 5G **43**
EX14: Hon 3E **33**
Questant La. EX10: Sidm 3E **37**
Quintet Cl. EX1: Hea 1G **17**

R

Rackclose La. EX4: Exe 1H **15** (4B **4**)
Rackfield Cotts. EX4: Exe 4F **9**
Rack St. EX1: Exe 1H **15** (4C **4**)
Raddenstile Ct. EX8: Exm 3D **46**
Raddenstile La. EX8: Exm 3D **46**
Radford Rd. EX2: Exe 1A **16** (5E **5**)
Radnor Pl. EX2: Exe 1B **16** (4F **5**)
Radway EX10: Sidm 5D **36**
Radway Cinema 5D 36
Ragg La. EX9: Bud S 5G **43**
Raglans EX2: Alp 6A **16**
Railway Cotts. EX1: Whip 6G **11**
Raleigh Cl. EX10: Sidm 2D **36**
Raleigh Ct. EX9: Bud S 3H **43**
Raleigh Ho. EX1: Exe 4G **5**
Raleigh Rd. EX1: Exe 1B **16** (3G **5**)
EX8: Exm 3C **46**
EX9: Bud S 3H **43**
EX11: Ott M 1E **31**
Rance Dr. EX8: Exm 4G **41**
Randell's Grn. EX8: Exm, Lit 3G **47**
RATSLOE 2A 6
Raven Cl. EX4: Penn 3A **10**
Rayleigh Pk. (Rugby Ground) 6D 40
Rayners EX6: Kennf 5A **20**
Read Cl. EX8: Exm 6E **41**
Rectory Cl. EX5: Whim 4A **26**
Rectory Dr. EX2: Alp 6H **15**
Rectory Gdns. EX3: Cly G 2A **24**
Redcliff Ct. EX9: Bud S 5G **43**
Red Cow Village EX4: Exe 4G **9**
Reddaway Dr. EX6: Exmin 3H **21**
REDHILLS 6E 9
Redhills EX4: Exe 5D **8**
EX9: Bud S 5G **43**
Redhills Cl. EX4: Exe 6E **9**
Redlands Cl. EX4: Whip 4E **11**
Redlands, The EX10: Sidm 6C **36**
Red Lion La. EX1: Exe 5B **10** (1F **5**)
Redvers Rd. EX4: Exe 1G **15**
Redwood Cl. EX8: Exm 4F **41**
EX14: Hon 5B **32**
Redwood Rd. EX10: Sidm 4D **36**
Regency Cres. EX8: Exm 3E **47**
Regents Ga. EX8: Exm 3D **46**
Regent's Pk. EX1: Hea 6C **10**
(not continuous)
Regent Sq. EX1: Hea 1D **16**
Regent St. EX2: Exe 3G **15**
Reme Dr. EX14: Hon 5B **32**
Rennes Dr. EX4: Penn 3A **10**
Rennes Ho. EX1: Whip 5F **11**
Renslade Ho. EX4: Exe 5B **4**
Retail Pk. Cl. EX2: Alp 3H **15**
Retreat Dr., The EX3: Top 2D **22**
Retreat Rd. EX3: Top 2E **23**
Rewe La. EX5: Whim 2A **28**
Rews Mdw. EX1: Pin 3B **12**
Rews Pk. Dr. EX1: Pin 3B **12**
Rexona Cl. EX2: Exe 4G **15**
Reynolds Cl. EX4: Pin 3H **11**
Ribston Av. EX1: Hea 6G **11**
Ribston Cl. EX1: Hea 6G **11**
Rices M. EX2: Exe 2G **15**
Richard Cl. EX8: Exm 5F **41**
Richmond Rd. EX4: Exe 6H **9** (2B **4**)
EX8: Exm 2F **47**
Ridge Way EX6: Ken 2B **44**
Ridgeway EX4: Cow 1G **9**
EX11: Ott M 1E **31**
EX14: Hon 5D **32**
Ridgeway Gdns. EX11: Ott M 1E **31**
Ridgeway Mead EX10: Sidm 2B **36**
Ridings, The EX3: Ebf 4A **24**
Rifford Rd. EX2: Won 2E **17**
Ringswell Av. EX1: Hea 6G **11**
Ringswell Pk. EX2: Won 1G **17**
Ripon Cl. EX4: Exe 6E **9**
River Front EX3: Ext 6H **23**
Rivermead Av. EX8: Exm 5C **40**
Rivermead Rd. EX2: Exe 3B **16**
Riverside *EX10: Sidm* *5D* ***36***
(off Riverside Rd.)
Riverside Cl. EX14: Hon 3D **32**
Riverside Ct. EX2: Exe 5D **4**
Riverside Leisure Cen. 2H 15 (6B 4)
Riverside Rd. EX3: Top 2E **23**
EX10: Sidm 5D **36**
Riverside Ter. *EX10: Sidm* *5D* ***36***
(off Riverside Rd.)
Riverside Vw. EX11: Ott M 2D **30**
Riversmeet EX3: Top 5G **23**
Rivers Wlk. EX2: C Wear 1C **22**
Riverview Dr. EX4: Exe 4F **9**
River Vw. Ter. EX6: Exmin 5B **22**
Riviera Ter. EX6: Exmin 5B **22**
Roberts Rd. EX2: Exe 1A **16** (5E **5**)
Robert Way EX10: New P 1D **34**
Roche Gdn. EX2: C Wear 6E **17**
Rockbeare Hill EX5: W Hill 5B **28**
Rockfield Ho. EX4: Exe 1E **5**
Rockside EX4: Exe 6G **9** (3A **4**)
Rockside Vs. EX4: Exe 6G **9** (2A **4**)
Rodney Cl. EX8: Lit 6A **42**
Rolle Barton EX9: Ott 4F **39**
Rolle Cotts. EX9: Bud S 3D **42**
Rolle Rd. EX8: Exm 3C **46**
EX9: Bud S 5G **43**
Rollestone Cres. EX4: Sto H 2C **10**
Rolle St. EX8: Exm 3C **46**
Rolle, The EX9: Bud S 5G **43**
Rolle Vs. EX8: Exm 3C **46**
Roly Poly Hill EX2: Exe, Ide 4E **15**
Roman Way EX14: Hon 2F **33**
Romsey Dr. EX2: Exe 1C **16** (5H **5**)
Rookwood Cl. EX14: Hon 3D **32**
Ropers Ct. EX9: Ott 4G **39**
Roper's La. EX9: Ott 4G **39**
Ropewalk Ho. EX8: Exm 3A **46**
Rosebank Cres. EX4: Sto H 3B **10**
Rosebarn Av. EX4: Sto H 3B **10**
Rosebarn La. EX4: Sto H 2B **10**
Rosebery Rd. EX4: Exe 4C **10**
EX8: Exm 1C **46**
Roseland Av. EX1: Hea 6E **11**
Roseland Cres. EX1: Hea 6E **11**
Roseland Dr. EX1: Hea 1E **17**
Roselands EX10: Sidm 5C **36**
Rosemary St. EX4: Exe 1F **15**
Rosemont Ct. EX2: Alp 5H **15**
Rosemount Cl. EX14: Hon 4D **32**
Rosemouth La. EX14: Hon 4C **32**
Rosemullion, The EX9: Bud S 5G **43**
Roseway EX8: Lit 1H **47**
Rosewell Cl. EX14: Hon 2F **33**
Rosewood Cres. EX5: Cly M 4G **19**
Rosewood Ter. EX4: Sto H 4B **10**
Ross Cl. EX1: Pin 3B **12**
Rougemont Castle 6A 10 (2D 4)
Rougemont Ct. EX6: Exmin 4H **21**
Roundball Cl. EX14: Hon 5E **33**
Roundball La. EX14: Hon 6D **32**
Roundhill Cl. EX4: Cow 1G **9**
Roundhouse La. EX8: Exm 5D **40**
Round Table Meet EX4: Sto H 3F **11**
Rowan Cl. EX14: Hon 5B **32**
Rowan Cft. EX1: Hea 6D **10**
Rowan Way EX4: Exe 5F **9**
Rowcroft Cl. EX14: Hon 4D **32**
Rowhorne Rd. EX4: Nadd 2A **8**

Sidmouth Rd.—Tidwell La.

Sidmouth Rd. EX5: Cly M .4D **18**
EX11: Ott M .2E **31**
EX14: Hon .5C **32**
Sidmouth Sports Cen. .2E 37
Sidmouth Swimming Pool .6D 36
Sid Pk. Rd. EX10: Sidm .4D **36**
Sid Rd. EX10: Sidm .5D **36**
Sid Va. Cl. EX10: Sidm .1F **37**
Sidwell St. EX4: Exe .6A **10** (2E **5**)
Sigford Rd. EX2: Alp .6B **16**
Signals, The EX5: Fen .1H **27**
Silverbirch Cl. EX2: Won .3E **17**
Silverdale EX8: Exm .4G **41**
Silver La. EX4: Exe .5B **10** (1G **5**)
Silvers, The EX3: Top .4B **18**
Silver St. EX11: Ott M .1D **30**
EX14: Hon .3E **33**
Silver Ter. EX4: Exe .6H **9** (2B **4**)
Silverton Rd. EX2: Alp .6B **16**
Simey Cl. EX4: Exe .5F **9**
Sir Alex Wlk. EX3: Top .2D **22**
Sivell Pl. EX2: Won .1D **16**
Slade Cl. EX11: Ott M .1F **31**
Slade Rd. EX11: Ott M .2F **31**
Sleap Hill EX9: E Bud .4E **39**
Sleepy Hollow *EX2: C Wear .1C* ***22***
(off Moonridge)
Slewton Cres. EX5: Whim .3A **26**
Slittercombe La. EX6: Ken .1B **44**
Small La. EX5: Broad .3E **7**
Smithfield Rd. EX2: Alp .6G **15**
Smiths Ct. EX2: Exe .2H **15**
Smythen St. EX1: Exe .1H **15** (4C **4**)
Snowdrop Cl. EX14: Hon .5C **32**
Snowdrop M. EX4: Exe .4D **8**
Solar Cres. EX4: Exe .2F **15**
Somerset Av. EX4: Exe .2E **15**
Somerville Cl. EX8: Exm .6F **41**
South Av. EX1: Hea .6C **10** (2H **5**)
Southbrook Rd. EX2: C Wear .4E **17**
Southernhay E. EX1: Exe .1A **16** (4D **4**)
Southernhay Gdns.
EX1: Exe .6A **10** (3E **5**)
Southernhay W. EX1: Exe .1A **16** (4E **5**)
(not continuous)
Southern Rd. EX8: Exm .1C **46**
Southern Wood EX8: Exm .5G **41**
Sth. Farm Rd. EX9: Bud S .3H **43**
South Ga. EX2: Exe .1A **16** (5D **4**)
Sth. Grange EX2: Sow .3H **17**
Southlands EX1: Hea .6C **10**
South Lawn EX10: Sidm .1E **37**
Sth. Lawn Ter. EX1: Hea .6D **10**
Sth. Parade EX9: Bud S .5H **43**
Southport Av. EX4: Exe .1E **15**
South St. EX1: Exe .6H **9** (3C **4**)
EX8: Exm .3C **46**
South Ter. EX8: Lymp .2B **40**
South Town EX6: Ken .1B **44**
Sth. View Ter. EX4: Sto H .4B **10**
EX6: Exmin .4B **22**
Southway EX10: Sidm .5E **37**
Sovereign Cl. EX8: Exm .6G **41**
Sovereign Ct. EX2: Sow .3H **17**
Sowden La. EX8: Exm, Lymp .3A **40**
SOWTON .6D **12**
Sowton Ind. Est. EX2: Sow .1A **18**
(not continuous)
Sowton La. EX5: Sow .5C **12**
Spacex Gallery .4C 4
Spencer Cl. EX8: Exm .5G **41**
Spencer Ct. *EX11: Ott M .2D* ***30***
(off St Saviours Rd.)
Spenser Av. EX2: Won .3D **16**
Spicer Rd. EX1: Exe .1B **16** (4F **5**)
Spider's La. EX8: Exm .4E **41**
Spindlewood Cl. EX14: Hon .6E **33**
Spinney Cl. EX2: Won .2G **17**
Spinning Path *EX4: Exe .5B* ***10***
(off Black Boy Rd.)
Spitup La. EX10: Sidm .2A **36**
Springfield Rd. EX4: Sto H .4B **10**
EX8: Exm .6D **40**
EX14: Hon .4G **33**
Spring Gdns. EX11: Ott M .2E **31**
Spruce Cl. EX4: Sto H .2F **11**
EX8: Exm .4F **41**
Spurway Hill EX6: Exmin .5H **21**
Square, The EX4: Exe .4F **9**
EX5: Whim .4A **26**
Staddon Cl. EX4: Whip .5F **11**
Stadium Way EX4: Exe .5B **10**
Staffick Cl. EX6: Ken .1B **44**
Stafford Rd. EX4: Exe .1F **15**
Stanford Rd. EX2: Won .1G **17**
Stanhope Dr. EX10: Sidm .3D **36**
Stanley M. EX9: Bud S .4G **43**
Stanley Sq. EX3: Top .4F **23**
Stanley Wlk. EX8: Exm .3F **41**
Stantyway Rd. EX9: Ott .6H **39**
Stanwey EX1: Hea .1E **17**
Staplake La. EX6: Star .2D **44**
Staplake Rd. EX6: Star .1F **45**
Staple's Bldgs. *EX8: Exm .2C* ***46***
(off Parade)
Staples M. *EX8: Exm .2C* ***46***
(off Exeter Rd.)
Star Barton La. EX4: Cow .1B **8**
STARCROSS .1F 45
Starcross Station (Rail) .1F 45
Station Rd. EX1: Pin .3A **12**
EX2: Ide .5C **14**
EX3: Ext .6A **24**
EX3: Top .3F **23**
EX4: Exe .4F **9**
EX5: Broad .5F **7**
EX5: Fen .1H **27**
EX6: Exmin .5C **22**
EX9: Bud S .4G **43**
EX10: New P .1D **34**
EX10: Sidm .4C **36**
Station Yd. EX4: Exe .6H **9** (2B **4**)
Steel Cl. EX14: Hon .3F **33**
Steeple Dr. EX2: Alp .1D **20**
Stepcote Hill EX1: Exe .1H **15** (4C **4**)
Stephen St. EX4: Exe .6A **10** (3D **4**)
Steps Cl. EX1: Pin .3B **12**
Steven's Cross Cl.
EX10: Sidm .1G **37**
Stevens La. EX10: Sidm .2C **36**
Stevenstone Rd. EX8: Exm .2F **47**
Stewart Cl. EX8: Exm .6G **41**
Stintway La. EX10: Sidm .5A **36**
Stocker Rd. EX4: Penn .3H **9**
STOKE HILL .3C **10**
Stoke Hill EX4: Sto H .3C **10**
Stoke Hill Cres. EX4: Sto H .3C **10**
Stokelyne EX8: Exm .6E **41**
Stoke Mdw. Cl. EX4: Sto H .2C **10**
Stoke Rd. EX4: Cow .1F **9**
Stokes Mead EX5: Wood .5G **25**
Stoke Valley Rd. EX4: Sto H .1A **10**
Stoneborough Ct. EX9: Bud S .4H **43**
Stoneborough La. EX9: Bud S .4H **43**
Stone Cl. EX14: Hon .5D **32**
Stone La. EX2: Exe .3G **15**
EX8: Lymp .2A **40**
Stone La. Retail Pk. EX2: Alp .3H **15**
Stoneyford Pk. EX9: Bud S .4H **43**
Stony La. EX5: Wood S .2G **25**
Stover Ct. EX1: Exe .5B **10** (1F **5**)
STOWFORD
Sidmouth .1A **36**
Budleigh Salterton .1C **38**
Stowford Ri. EX10: Sidm .2B **36**
Strand EX3: Top .4F **23**
EX8: Exm .3C **46**
Strand Ct. EX3: Top .4F **23**
Strand, The EX6 .1F **45**
EX8: Lymp .2A **40**
Strand Vw. EX3: Top .4F **23**
Stratford Av. EX4: Whip .4G **11**
Strawberry Av. EX2: Alp .6A **16**
Strawberry Hill EX8: Lymp .2A **40**
Strawberry La. EX11: Ott M .3B **30**
Stream Ct. EX2: Exe .2H **15** (6C **4**)
Streamers Mdws. EX14: Hon .4E **33**
Streatham Dr. EX4: Penn .4G **9**
Streatham Ri. EX4: Penn .4G **9**
Streatham Sports Cen. .3H 9
STRETE RALEGH .1C **28**
Stuart Rd. EX1: Hea .6D **10**
Sturges Rd. EX8: Exm .1F **47**
Sullivan Rd. EX2: Won .1G **17**
Summer Cl. EX4: Whip .4F **11**
EX8: Lit .1G **47**
Summerfield EX5: Wood .4G **25**
EX10: Sidm .1D **36**
Summerland EX14: Hon .4E **33**
Summerland Ga. *EX1: Exe .6B* ***10*** *(2F* ***5****)*
(off Belgrave Rd.)
Summerland St. EX1: Exe .5B **10** (1F **5**)
Summer La. EX4: Sto H, Whip .3F **11**
EX8: Exm .4C **40**
Summerway EX4: Whip .4F **11**
Sunhill Av. EX3: Top .2F **23**
Sunhill La. EX3: Top .2F **23**
Sunnyfield EX5: Broad .3E **7**
Sunnyhill EX11: Ott M .1E **31**
Sunnymoor Cl. EX1: Pin .3B **12**
Sunwine Pl. EX8: Exm .3D **46**
Surbiton Cres. EX4: Exe .2F **15**
Sussex Cl. EX4: Exe .2E **15**
Swains Ct. EX3: Top .3E **23**
Swains Rd. EX9: Bud S .3H **43**
Swallow Ct. EX4: Exe .4F **9**
Swallow Dr. EX2: Wheat .3D **14**
Swallowfield Rd. EX2: C Wear .4E **17**
Swan Ct. EX2: Exe .2B **16** (6F **5**)
Swan Rd. EX6: Star .2E **45**
Swan Yd. EX4: Exe .1G **15** (5A **4**)
Sweetbrier La. EX1: Hea .6E **11**
Swiss Cl. EX8: Exm .4D **40**
Sycamore Cl. EX1: Hea .1F **17**
EX5: Broad .4F **7**
EX8: Exm .5G **41**
EX14: Hon .5C **32**
Sydenham Ho. EX1: Exe .1H **5**
Sydney Pl. EX2: Exe .6B **4**
Sydney Rd. EX2: Exe .2G **15**
Sylvan Av. EX4: Sto H .3B **10**
Sylvan Cl. EX8: Exm .5C **40**
Sylvania Dr. EX4: Sto H .2C **10**
Sylvan Rd. EX4: Sto H .3B **10**
Synagogue Pl. EX4: Exe .6H **9** (3C **4**)

T

Taddiforde Rd. EX4: Exe .5G **9**
Taddyforde Ct. EX4: Exe .4G **9**
Taddyforde Ct. Mans. EX4: Exe .4G **9**
Taddyforde Est. EX4: Exe .4G **9**
Tamarisk Cl. EX4: Sto H .2F **11**
Tan La. EX2: Exe .3H **15**
Tape La. EX14: Hon .3A **32**
Tappers Cl. EX3: Top .3F **23**
Taps Cl. EX6: Exmin .4B **22**
Tarbet Av. EX1: Hea .5D **10**
Taunton Cl. EX2: Exe .3G **15**
Tavistock Rd. EX4: Exe .5G **9** (1A **4**)
Taylor Cl. EX11: Ott M .1B **30**
Teazle Ct. EX2: Exe .1H **15** (5C **4**)
Tedburn Rd. EX4: Wheat .6A **8**
Tedstone La. EX8: Lymp .1C **40**
Telegraph La. EX5: W Hill .3D **28**
Telford Rd. EX4: Exe .5G **9** (1A **4**)
Temple Gdns. EX10: Sidm .4D **36**
Temple Rd. EX2: Exe .1A **16** (5E **5**)
Temple St. EX10: Sidm .4D **36**
Tennyson Av. EX2: Won .3D **16**
Tennyson Way EX8: Exm .3E **41**
Thackeray Rd. EX4: Whip .4G **11**
Thelma Hulbert Gallery, The .3D 32
Third Av. EX1: Hea .6D **10**
EX2: C Wear .1C **22**
EX2: Won .1H **17**
Thomas Cl. EX8: Exm .3E **41**
Thompson Rd. EX1: Hea .5E **11**
Thornberry Av. EX1: Hea .6F **11**
Thorn Cl. EX1: Hea .6F **11**
Thorndale Ct. EX4: Exe .4D **8**
Thorne Farm Way EX11: Ott M .1C **30**
Thornfield Cl. EX8: Exm .5C **40**
Thornlea EX4: Exe .5H **9**
Thornpark Ri. EX1: Hea .6F **11**
Thornton Cl. EX9: Bud S .5G **43**
Thornton Hill EX4: Exe .4A **10**
Thorntree Bus. Units EX8: Exm .6H **41**
Thorpe Av. EX8: Exm .4D **40**
Threecorner Pl. EX2: Alp .6A **16**
Thurlow Rd. EX4: Sto H .4C **1**
Tidwell Cl. EX9: Bud S .3G **4**
Tidwell La. EX9: Bud S, E Bud .1G **4**

62 A-Z Exeter